AF557837

INDIANS AT HEROD'S GATE

INDIANS AT HEROD'S GATE

A Jerusalem Tale

NAVTEJ SARNA

Published in Rainlight by
Rupa Publications India Pvt. Ltd 2014
7/16, Ansari Road, Daryaganj
New Delhi 110002

Sales Centres:
Bengaluru Chennai
Hyderabad Jaipur Kathmandu
Kolkata Mumbai Prayagraj

P-ISBN: 978–81–291-3451-6
E-ISBN: 978-81-291-3440-0

Fifth impression 2024

10 9 8 7 6 5

Printed in India

Dedicated

to

the proud Indian at Herod's Gate,

Sheikh Mohammad Munir Ansari

OLD CITY OF JERUSALEM
CHRISTIAN QUARTER
MOSLEM QUARTER
ARMENIAN QUARTER
JEWISH QUARTER
Legend
Road
Hotel
Synagogue
Museum
Church
19 Site
Mosque
Parking
0
100m
200m
Scale - 1:5,500
18 DAMASCUS GATE
33 HEROD'S GATE
40 LION'S GATE
26 GOLDEN GATE
21 DUNG GATE
68 ZION GATE
36 JAFFA GATE
47 NEW GATE
Dome of the Rock 20
Mt. Moriah Temple Mount 62
Haram al-Sharif
23 El-Aqsa Mosque
Church of the Holy Sepulcher
VIA DOLOROSA
Western Wall
The Citadel 17
David's Tower 19
Cathedral of St. James
Cardo Gallery
St. Ann Ch.
Indian Hospice 35
Rockefeller Museum

Contents

Prologue

Indian Hospice

Yesterday, it rained so hard
Lemons spilt from the lemon tree
And rolled over cobble stones in my Jerusalem courtyard.

I thought of Baba Farid
Who came on a pilgrimage centuries ago.
In a hole cut from rock by the room where I sleep,

He stood for forty days and nights
Without food or drink. Nothing for him was strange
In the way his body slipped into a hole in the ground,

And nothing was not.
Rust in the stones and blood at the rim of his tongue.
In the humming dark

He heard bird beaks stitching webs of dew,
Sharp hiss of breath let out from a throat,
Whose throat he did not know.

Was it his mother crying O Farid, where are you now?
It's what she did when he swung
Up and down, knees in a mango tree,

Head in the mouth of a well,
Singing praises to God.
Crawling out of his hole, welts on his cheeks,

And underfoot in bedrock—visionary recalcitrance.
A lemon tree wobbled in a high wind.
Under it, glistening in its own musk, the black iris of Abu Dis.

Wild with the scents of iris and lemon he sang—O Farid
This world is a muddy garden,
Stone, fruit and flesh all flaming with love.

Meena Alexander
(*Birthplace with Buried Stones*)

I

Hill of Evil Counsel

I could have begun this account at the Mount of Olives, whose graves, forever waiting for the Messiah to raise the dead from their slumber, are bathed even now in the warm light of the sinking sun. Instead I find myself standing on the Hill of Evil Counsel. Its name is diabolical, irresistible. Here it was that two thousand years ago, the High Priest Caiaphas and his colleagues decided to arrest Jesus and gave Judas the thirty pieces of silver that would be the price of his betrayal.

I look at the stunning vista that spreads below this promenade on the escarpment that runs to the edge of the gardens of the old Government House, once the residence of the British high commissioner in the days of the Mandate, and the UN's headquarters in Jerusalem since 1948. A smoky twilight is settling down in the lightly wooded valley just below me, which unfolds gently from this Hill but rises more sharply on the far side towards Mount Zion. This is the valley of Hinnom, or Gehinnom, or Jahannam. Or simply, Hell. Nasir-i Khusrau, the Persian traveller of a thousand years ago, wrote: '[T]he common people state that when you stand at the brink of the valley you may hear the cries of those in hell, which come up from below. I myself went up there to listen, but heard nothing.'

Where the two valleys meet I can barely discern the site of the city of David, an ancient settlement from the Bronze Age, once fed by the springs of Gihon and now covered by the Palestinian township of Silvan. In the far reaches of the narrow Kidron Valley, at the base of the Mount of Olives, I can make out the faintly glistening five golden onion domes of the Orthodox Russian church of St Mary Magdalene, each adorned with its Orthodox cross. The church opens for severely restricted hours but I have managed to see its meditative nuns walking, hunched in their habits, in the shadowy green surroundings of the white sandstone building marked by arches and gabled roofs. Just one twisting street below is the Garden of Gethsemane, where an exhausted Jesus was arrested, as he rested under the olive trees. The descendants of those trees, their trunks swollen with centuries, their shoulders burdened with having seen too much, are still there. Next to the olive grove is the grand Church of All Nations, said to enshrine a piece of bedrock where Jesus prayed alone on the night before his arrest.

The Old City, with its walls built by the Ottoman sultan, Suleiman the Magnificent, five hundred years ago, rises out of these two valleys, as if out of an abyss. Houses scramble up the slopes of the valleys, roads snake into their depths. And beyond the Old City spread the proud buildings of West Jerusalem, each made of the same stone.

The lights begin to come up in the windows one by one and at this hour it is not possible, nor necessary, to figure out which light is Israeli and Arab and which stone is holy to the Christians, or the Jews, or the Muslims.

At this hour of the lighting of the lamps, it is difficult to imagine the desert wilderness that all this must have been, not that very long ago. When the bleak paths that came from Damascus and Jaffa, Bethlehem and Hebron, would have led the caravans of travellers, happy and relieved to see Jerusalem's walls after surviving weeks of hostilities of nature and raids of bandits, to one or the other gates of the Old City. All manner of travellers and adventurers, pilgrims and priests, Jews of every hue, Christian Crusaders, Islamic warriors, drawn to this lodestone helplessly.

And even more difficult is to imagine a time before these Ottoman walls. A time of Abraham and Isaac, David and Solomon. A time of other walls that have long been buried under the dust, that show up only tantalizingly in some archaeological dig, enabling some heat-crazed archaeologist to die in peace, one more line added to some obscure map. In some other city, those old stones may be carried away, used to build some peasant hut, or serve as a rough step, or be chipped away and thrown by careless boys. But here, each stone that is unearthed is a piece of history, a triumphant political statement, an affirmation or a decrial, one more microscopic addition to the jumbled jigsaw of kingdoms—temporal and spiritual—that is Jerusalem.

The seventeenth-century Turkish traveller Evliya Çelebi, who travelled twice through Palestine in his wanderings through thirty countries, is my observant guide on many walks through this land; his first sentence on Jerusalem says it all: 'It is called in Greek the Province of Aelia, in Syriac Maqdisha, in Hebrew Has, and in Arabic Beit-ul Maqdis or Quds. It contains the shrines of one hundred and twenty four thousand Prophets. Before and after the deluge it was the qibla of mankind.' The city, after all, is said to have seventy names. One finds mention, four thousand years ago, of a town named Ursalim. Etymologies of Jerusalem abound: that which is founded by Shalem, the ancient god of the evening star; a combination of 'Yireh' (awe/God will see to it) and 'shalem' or 'shalom' (peace); the Abode of Peace and so on. All agree, however, that it is holiness that marks this city; holy to the three Abrahamic religions. Jerusalem in that way is as much of the heavens as it is of earth, as much about historical facts as about faith.

The sun is sinking fast and the rich yellow light is weakening, able to catch less and less in its faltering grasp. Only the tops of trees on this Hill—the pines and the olives through which rustles a cool breeze—and the golden Dome of the Rock, in the centre of the massive platform atop Mount Moriah, the platform that the Jews call Har haBáyit or the Temple Mount and the Muslims call Haram al-Sharif or the Noble Sanctuary—the place which concentrates within itself a world of conflict, a sea of faith, history and fable, longings and aspirations—remain visible. It is on that Dome that the eye always settles when looking upon Jerusalem, as it rises above the platform of ageless flagstones. That is, according to so many prophets, where it all began—where Adam was created; where Abraham nearly sacrificed his son Isaac; where David placed the Ark of the Covenant, the foundation stone of Solomon's Temple, the place from where Mohammed went on his night journey to the heavens. So I watch it as the sun sets and as the rays of light shorten. The burnished gold of the Dome seems to grow brighter, as if it is gathering the rays within itself, to exude them all night at will.

To find Herod's Gate I have to go to the other side of the Old City, to its northern wall. Beyond this wall lies the crowded commercial centre of Arab East Jerusalem, pierced by Salahdin Street with its shops, internet cafés and small hotels. The crowded pavements, where fresh kababs are roasted next to mounds of shoes and underwear, give the whole place the bustling look of an Arab market, very unlike the quiet, orderly streets of Jewish West Jerusalem. On this side lie the buildings of the American Colony and the houses of the Jerusalem notables that came up in the late nineteenth and early twentieth centuries.

It is difficult on any day, and impossible on a Friday, for a car to navigate the road that separates the Old City from this neighbourhood or to find a break in the constant stream of pedestrians, women in hijab and men in keffiyehs, many with walking canes, heading into the Old City to pray at the Al-Aqsa Mosque on the Haram, the third holiest of Muslim religious sites.

I look for flower-sellers as I enter Herod's Gate; it has also been known as Bab al- Zahira or the Gate of Flowers down the centuries. Instead there are fruit-sellers lining its substantial archway. It is the beginning of March; the last pomegranates, the early oranges, watermelons and melons are piled up inside the gate. As I enter the archway I am greeted by a compact man of medium height, with alert, grey eyes and a polite, easy and genuine smile.

'I am Nazeer,' he says, 'Nazeer Ansari.'

Quickly, he leads me through the gate and up a few steps that rise from the gate into the street inside the Old City. Before I have had time to look around, I find myself staring awestruck at a green iron gate with its two stone pillars. The words 'Indian Hospice' are carved on one of them and on the other, in Arabic, 'Zawiya al-Hindiya'. An indescribable excitement grips me: an Indian presence in the middle of old Jerusalem. Nazeer smiles at my surprise and opens the gate.

'You are in India now,' he says as we start walking up the broad path from the gate. Tall saru trees with their tight pine cones line both sides of the path. 'My father is waiting for you.'

I look up. At the end of that path of broad steps stands a tall, erect man, dressed elegantly in an overcoat with a woollen scarf around his neck, a soft, peaked woollen cap protecting his head.

Finally, several months after I first heard mention of this place, I am about to meet Sheikh Mohammad Munir Ansari, director of the Indian Hospice.

'You are welcome,' Sheikh Munir takes my hand warmly in both his hands. When we get to know each other better, he will always embrace me, thrice, Arab style. We stand for a few minutes at the entrance to the hospice. I try to gauge his age. He looks younger than the eighty he turns out to be. He smiles easily and the eyes behind the gold-rimmed glasses are lively. Behind us a steady stream of Palestinian women and children are coming up the path and entering a complex of two buildings that seems part of the hospice.

'Those buildings are the UNRWA clinic,' Sheikh Munir says by way of explanation in his clear, deliberate manner. 'For the refugees of 1948. This building,' he points towards a part of the clinic, 'was built by Indian soldiers during the Second World War. It is called the Delhi wing. And this,' he points to his left, 'is where we live now: the Travancore wing. It was also built by the soldiers.'

As if on cue, the gate to the Travancore wing opens and a tall woman steps out. She is stylishly dressed in trousers and high heels and her hair is pulled back in a French knot. Confidently, she extends a hand to greet me. Her eyes shine with the same elemental playfulness that I have seen in her father's face.

'This is my eldest daughter, Najam,' the sheikh introduces us. 'And this,' he points to another smartly dressed lady who comes out of another door, 'is my other daughter, Nourjahan.'

'You can call me Jani, everybody does,' she introduces herself.

'And this,' Nazeer adds, pointing to a third lady who has joined us, 'is my Wafa, my dear wife.'

I don't know it then, but this is going to be the pattern of so many meetings: Nazeer outside, his father at the top of the steps, and then the ladies in the house...

Together we enter a short narrow corridor with its chequerboard of black and white mosaic tiles. A large map of the old city of Jerusalem fills one wall.

'This is a rare map from the early twentieth century,' Nazeer points out. 'On this you can see the city as it was before the takeover of 1967. You can see how close the houses were to the Wailing

Wall. After '67 they were all cleared up. And this, on the right, is our office.'

The office is a small room with a large writing desk behind which stands a large Indian flag. Iconic photos of Gandhi and Nehru adorn the walls surrounded by several small ones.

'This is my father,' Sheikh Munir points at one of them, 'with Maulana Muhammad Ali of the Khilafat. And here is he alone, with a different turban, the Indian one.'

I take a quick look at the photos of the tall bespectacled Indian figure, the elder Sheikh Nazir Ansari of Saharanpur. But this, I realize, is not the time to ask about his story; there will be time enough. So we step out into the sunlit courtyard of the hospice, where the women are waiting, making idle talk around a grove of lemon and orange trees. It's a pleasant young sun of early March in which I enjoy the little orange that Najam hands me. I can bite right into it and eat it, peel and all. A small mosque opens out into the courtyard and, through its half-open door, I can see the bare room with its arched walls and a mihrab. A full carpet covers its floor. On the far end of the courtyard are a number of rooms, several in a state of dereliction. Sheikh Munir points out two graves—perhaps of pilgrims or earlier sheikhs—that mark the furthest end. A visitor's room contains more photographs, and a table with a visitor's book with details of people who have stayed at the hospice in recent years.

Finally, I ask the question that has brought me here.

'Why is this known as Baba Farid's hospice?'

'You are right, this is also called the "Zawiya al-Faridiya". They say Baba Farid came here from India, meditated here, and then his followers began to come and stay here. A long time ago. They were given a waqf, first the mosque and those two rooms. And then the property expanded through the centuries as a place for Indian pilgrims to stay.'

Sheikh Munir leads me to one of the rooms at the far end of the courtyard. An attendant brings out a bunch of keys and unlocks a low door. I have to bend to step in. Cobwebs flutter in the sunlight that streams in and a dank smell rises from within. He points towards an opening in the floor, barely visible at the far end of the room.

'There are some rooms below this room,' Sheikh Munir says. 'It is believed that those are the rooms where Baba Farid meditated. And in this room my wife and children hid when the bombs fell here in 1967 and the Israeli soldiers entered the hospice.'

It is our first meeting, so I do not push for details. But I know that I must know.

In the long drawing room in the Travancore wing, I meet the sheikh's wife, Ikram. She speaks little but her presence is pleasing. There is tea, Indian style. 'Lipton is the best,' someone says. And 'bourekas', fresh pastries stuffed with spinach and cheese, and carrot cake and poppyseed cake. Each of the women has made something and wants me to taste it. There is even a fruit salad. 'This is a French salad, in the name of Nimala, our sister who lives in Switzerland,' Nazeer explains. Someone mentions that on occasions like this they miss Nazer, the eldest brother who lives in Saudi Arabia.

They are a graceful and charming family and I hate to tear myself away. But there is much I need to know and for weeks I know I will obsess about this little Indian corner in the Old City, about the underground chamber of Baba Farid, about Indian soldiers during the World War, about shells raining down on children huddled in a dark, dank room, about the man who came here mysteriously from Saharanpur, and the family that laughs and smiles and teases one another.

2

Spies, Diplomats, Authors and Romantics

Dusk is falling and the shop shutters are coming down as I walk back from Herod's Gate towards the American Colony Hotel down Salahdin Street, past the old stone houses of Arab Jerusalem's notables, past the private cemetery where many members of the illustrious Husseini family lie buried under the tall trees.

The American Colony Hotel lies just east of the fault line between East and West Jerusalem. A hundred metres away, from 1948 to 1967, used to run the barbed wires of No Man's Land between Israel and Jordan. Two different worlds carried on their daily lives separated by the barbed wire, a concrete wall built by the Jordanians and the occasional landmine. Two eminent men whom I got to know and admire immensely have written of their childhoods in this divided Jerusalem: the Palestinian philosopher Professor Sari Nusseibeh and the famous Israeli writer Amoz Oz, who grew up on either side of the divide, separated only by destiny and a few hundred metres.

Nusseibeh's childhood home was just across the road from the American Colony, a house with 'Persian carpets, gold-embossed academic degrees on the wall, crystal decanters for after-dinner drinks, and dozens of finely buffed tennis trophies.' From this house the young Sari would stare across the rock and thistle of No Man's Land and the forbidden territory that lay beyond, at the strange-looking buses and knots of bearded Orthodox Jews with black coats and dangling side curls who inhabited the religious Haredim neighbourhood of Mea Shearim. His young imagination was fired by what he had heard about the other side: 'the elegant shops on Jaffa Road, the Gary Cooper Westerns at the Edison Cinema, the villas in the old neighbourhoods, and how from the hills to the west you could see the Mediterranean.' On 25 December, Sari would make his way to the nearby Mandelbaum Gate, 'Jerusalem's Checkpoint Charlie', which would open only on Christmas day to allow pilgrims from the other side to visit the Church of the Holy Sepulchre.

From the other side, Amos Oz's exceptional imagination would allow him to

> ...stare wide-eyed at the other Jerusalem: a city of old cypress trees that were more black than green; streets of stone walls, interlaced grills, cornices and dark walls; the alien, silent, aloof, shrouded Jerusalem; the Abyssinian, Muslim, pilgrim, Ottoman city, the strange missionary city of crusaders and Templars; the Greek, Armenian, Italian, brooding, Anglican, Greek Orthodox city; the monastic, Coptic, Catholic, Lutheran, Scottish, Sunni, Shi'ite, Sufi, Alawite city, swept by the sound of bells and the wail of the muezzin, thick with pine trees, frightening yet alluring, with all its concealed enchantments, its warrens of narrow streets that were forbidden to us and threatened us out of the darkness; a secretive, malign city pregnant with disaster.

The barbed wire was rolled up many years ago and all of Jerusalem annexed by Israel, but the virtual barrier between east and west still remains. One has only to turn into Nablus Road towards the

American Colony Hotel to know that one is in the Arab east; there is something in the air that leaves no doubt.

Playing with these thoughts I step into the hotel, once the home of a Husseini notable and his four wives, and then of the Spaffords, an American Christian evangelical family that moved to Jerusalem sometime towards the end of the nineteenth century. Aided by Swiss consultants, the descendants of the family turned the house into the famous hotel. Every romantic, tragic or historic figure of the Middle East from T.E. Lawrence to Churchill to Glubb Pasha appears to have stayed there, not to mention people like Bob Dylan, Peter O'Toole and John Steinback. Understandably, it is now a gathering hole, as a newspaper article colourfully put it, of spies, diplomats, authors and romantics. It is doused in old-world colonial charm with its history all pinned up in pictures and news clippings on the walls. Besides which it has a well-stocked bookshop and an even better stocked bar. During the winter months the bar is tucked away into a cosy cellar, and in the summer it moves out into the scented garden.

The bookshop is run by Munther Fahmi, a Palestinian American of infinite charm. On my several trips to Jerusalem he was the first person I would stop to meet—for a cup of Arabic coffee, for a browse through his shelves, for a conversation that inevitably revealed some new angle or, if not, at least brought a smile. His straw hat at a rakish angle on his head, green-framed spectacles in hand, he mixed easily with foreign correspondents and diplomats. A few minutes of conversation and he would, with an uncanny ability, pick out just the book for you, a book that you would be hard put to refuse. It was a rare occasion when I walked out of his shop without buying something or the other—a book, a Palestine poster, a Moleskine notebook. Such was his charm. And he was never short on the one-liners: one day when I offered him chewing gum he responded, 'No thank you, I am Catholic.'

It's too early to go to bed so I head towards Munther's bookshop across the courtyard. The shop is doing brisk business.

'You are open late tonight,' I say.

'Yesterday I was open till ten thirty at night; I hope it will be even later today. Now it is too hot for people to come and buy books during the day.'

I beat him to the question.

'Drink?' I ask.

He hesitates a moment and then quickly makes a decision. He signals to his dark-eyed shop assistant.

'Hanna, will you?'

She takes his seat behind the counter and we walk into the garden.

A boy in a black T-shirt is lighting the little tea lights on each table. The call for the Maghrib prayer of the evening rises from the mosque just behind the hotel. It floats along with the pleasant breeze, over the low tables with their usual mix of foreign correspondents, diplomats and representatives of international agencies who lounge among the bushes, glasses of draft beer and red wine between them. It is pleasant to sit there with him and distinguish the scents rising from the bushes and trees—sage, rosemary, pine; the one that has the capacity to push away all others is lavender. It will stay on my hand for a long time because I accidentally brushed a bush as I pushed back my chair.

It is in this garden bar, surrounded by this celebration of herbal scents, that I manage to scrape through Nazeer's formal politeness one evening.

'We have to write this story, Nazeer. Your father's story.'

'What is the plan?' he asks, playing for time.

'No plan. A simple story: your father, his father, the Indian Hospice. How it all began, what happened during the centuries and if we can, what happened during your father's lifetime...'

He doesn't take long to make up his mind.

'I will help you,' he says. 'You will have my full cooperation.'

We shake on it over the low table with its wavering tea light. And he soon goes home, his quick, short steps echoing down the darkening Salahdin Street. I don't know then how he will help me, but I learn later from his wife and sisters that our little conversation in the twilit garden bar changed the pattern of his life for months. He began to steal time from the family, spending it in winning the trust of the librarian at the Islamic University of Abu Dis, an Arab town just beyond the Mount of Olives, where the old records of the sharia court are kept in file cabinets on wheels. And he stayed up many nights, sifting through the documents he found, struggling with the Ottoman Arabic, picking out the slightest reference to the Indian Hospice. And every once in a while, he found a little odd-shaped piece that fitted in the large jigsaw puzzle called the past.

3

'The Door to His Hospice Was Never Closed'

Farida, with your prayer mat on your shoulder,
Your coarse robe around your neck
Your words appear sweet but you hide a dagger in your heart
Outwardly you appear bright but your heart is dark as night.

In this verse Baba Farid or, more properly, Sheikh Farid ud-din Masud Ganj-i-Shakar, criticizes the hypocritical holy men who wandered through Punjab in India during his time. This spiritual heir of Moinuddin Chisti and Sheikh Bakhtiar Kaki established the Chisti Sufi order in Punjab. His thought and writing, which would give birth to the Punjabi literary tradition, would also influence many masters who would follow him including Guru Nanak, the founder of the Sikh faith. A number of Baba Farid's verses, including the one quoted above, are to be found in the Granth Sahib, the holy book of the Sikhs.

'Baba Farid came here many centuries ago…' Sheikh Munir had said.

And Nanak too was an indefatigable traveller. The floating thought is tantalizing: Nanak came to Mecca and Medina in the early fifteenth century, and it is known that he returned to Hindustan via Baghdad. Given the fact that he was set on visiting spiritual centres to meet holy men, would it be too unreasonable to presume that he may have come to Jerusalem too? It was not after all an untrodden path. Baba Farid had already been there and so had thousands of other Indian pilgrims in his wake, on their way to or returning from the hajj, taking the boat to Basra and then following the land route to Mecca through Damascus or Jerusalem. And if Nanak did come here then where else would he go to except where I have just been, the place where Baba Farid, the man whose verses he knew, had meditated. It's a mesmerizing thought and a strange shiver takes hold of me. In Jerusalem, these connections, more of the soul than anything else, seem entirely possible.

But I know that it will be impossible to find a piece of paper, or unearth a stone tablet, that will provide proof. So perhaps I must leave that by-lane unexplored and go back to the journey of Baba Farid from the hot plains of twelfth-century Punjab to the precincts of this ancient city, already then holy to three faiths, already then seeped in blood.

I wonder where that story should begin.

Perhaps on that day, 2 October 1187, when Sultan Salah al-Din, known now to the world as Saladin, entered Jerusalem as conqueror, winning the city back for Islam after nearly a century of Crusader rule. It was an auspicious day. Muslims were celebrating the miraculous night journey of Prophet Mohammed. This was the night when, according to Muslim belief, the Prophet had been woken up by the archangel Gabriel and had flown on his white steed Al-Buraq to the remote mosque (later identified as the Al-Aqsa Mosque in Jerusalem). Thence he had risen to the heavens from the rock on the Haram al-Sharif on a ladder of the finest gold. On this journey he had met God on His throne and all the earlier prophets including Abraham, Moses and Jesus. It was also then that he came back with the command that Muslims would pray five times a day.

Saladin was wise as he was brave. He took the city peacefully, resisting the temptation to seek revenge for the way the Crusaders had acted when they had taken the city ninety years earlier. Then the slaughter of Muslims had continued for three days, and according to an eyewitness, 'in the Temple and the Porch of Solomon, men rode in blood up to their knees and bridle-reins.' Saladin wanted the city intact, including the Al-Aqsa Mosque and the Dome of the Rock, and not burnt down by the fleeing Christians.

So not a single man was killed and generous terms of surrender were set. The barons were allowed to ransom themselves—and that too cheaply—and the poor, taken as prisoners of war, were freed in large numbers; it is said that Saladin could not bear the weeping of the families. Some historians would not take kindly to Saladin's mercy; he allowed the Christians to retain a foothold in Palestine and a third Crusade followed, led by Richard I of England and Philip II of France. Though they would not be able to retake Jerusalem—the city would remain in Muslim hands for the next seven hundred and thirty years—a Frank presence was established in a thin strip on the Mediterranean coast, all the way from Beirut to Jaffa.

But in that moment of triumph in 1187, Saladin had plans to make Jerusalem a truly Muslim city again. The most essential step was to cleanse the religious places, most particularly the Haram al-Sharif itself, of the Christian elements introduced by the Crusaders. The statues that had been installed in the Dome of the Rock (called the Temple of the Lord during the Crusader years) were removed and the hidden inscriptions from the Quran revealed once again. The Crusaders had covered up the rock with a marble plaque and put a Christian altar on it, partly to prevent their own priests from giving away pieces of the rock to pilgrims as holy mementoes. Saladin had this plaque removed to reveal the rock once again; the beautifully crafted iron railing put around the rock by the Crusaders was left intact and is now preserved in a museum. The Al-Aqsa Mosque too had to be severely overhauled. It had become the home of the Templars, so called because they had offered to help guard the paths to Jerusalem against bandits and had been given housing close to the Temple. They had partitioned the Aqsa, created a refectory, added a chapel and bricked up the mihrab. All this was reversed by Saladin. As the second caliph, Omar, had done when he conquered Jerusalem for Islam in AD 638, Saladin too worked with his men to wash the massive platform and the corridors of the Haram with rose water. Finally the mosque was once again ready for Muslim prayers after almost a century.

Saladin also began to Islamize buildings and property beyond the immediate surrounding of the Haram. He confiscated the residence of the patriarch next to the Holy Sepulchre and took over the Convent of St Anna, converting it into a madrasa. As part of his effort to keep out Shia influence, he converted properties into Sufi 'khanqahs'—open houses for pilgrims—and madrasas. His aim was not to simply encourage local Sunnis, for those he considered influenced unduly by Shia ideology. He wanted to attract Sunni Muslims from other lands. Sufis, dervishes and scholars would start moving to Jerusalem to savour again the holy breeze of a land that had remained so long in enemy hands. Many of them, in the centuries to come, would be from India. And one of them, perhaps among the first, would be Baba Farid.

The other strand of the story begins not too far from Jerusalem, only down the road so to speak, in Damascus. But then it takes a long loop, all the way to India, before swinging back. In the tenth century, Abu Ishaq Shami, tired of the intrigue and materialism of the Damascene court, found his way to the village of Chist, near the Afghan city of Herat. He was to found the Chisti 'silsila' of Sufis. One of his disciples, perhaps a generation or two removed, was Usman Harwani, a respected dervish in the city of Harwan in Persia. Harwani had one day accepted a young disciple by the name of Moinuddin of Nishapur. It was the same city in which another man—Omar Khayyam—had sold his fruit orchard and set out on the road in search of learning and spiritual guidance.

Moinuddin spent the next twenty years travelling as Harwani's disciple, discoursing with religious and spiritual men, exploring the world of mysticism. When the time came to take leave of his mentor, Moinuddin took the name of Chisti from the founder of the school and proceeded towards India, where he hoped to unlock the secrets of the spirit. Somewhere along the way, he accepted a young Afghan, Qutubuddin Bakhtiar Kaki, as his disciple.

Moinuddin Chisti laid the roots of the Chisti silsila in India based on the principles of contentment and compassion, abandonment and abnegation, generosity and truthfulness. After living and preaching in Multan and Lahore, he settled down in Ajmer. Here his simple house became the centre for gatherings based on the principles of humanity, where the poor and rich were welcomed alike, irrespective of caste or religion, and ate together from the open kitchen. In the evenings they all came together in the 'sama' or concert where the 'zikr' was performed through the rhythmic repetition of the name of God, to the accompaniment of music. This tradition of music—some would call it un-Islamic but one that comes so naturally in India—is prevalent till this day, most visibly in the qawwalis sung at his dargah in Ajmer or at those of his latter-day followers, Nizamuddin Auliya in Delhi and Salim Chisti in Fatehpur Sikri near Agra. Music and mystical poetry, be they of the Sufis, the Bhaktas or of Guru Nanak, are the vehicles by which these great souls imparted the message of the True Word, the praise of the Divine. While Moinuddin stayed for the most part in Ajmer, his disciple Kaki moved to Delhi where he began to command a huge spiritual gathering, including the Slave King Iltutmish. Kaki's closest disciple was young Farid.

Farid was born on the first day of Ramadan in 1173 in the Punjab town of Kothiwal in a family that could trace its lineage to Caliph Omar. The legend goes that it was a cloudy night and people had no way of finding out if Ramadan had begun or not. A dervish then said that a great soul had been born and the people must look to him for their answer. If the child drank milk then Ramadan had still not begun. As it happened, the child Farid refused his mother's breast, and the people knew that it was the first day of Ramadan.

Several stories explain how he got the name of Shakar Ganj or Ganj-i-Shakar. One goes back to the time his mother, Bibi Miriam, taught him to pray. When he enquired what it would get him, she replied that he would get sugar. She would hide a lump of sugar under the prayer carpet and hand it to him when he completed his prayers. One day she forgot to put the sugar but yet it appeared after the prayers. From that day on, she started calling her son Shakar Ganj, and that was how he would be revered for centuries. Another story talks of the time when, as a young man given to rigorous abstinence in worship, he fasted for three days. Finally overwhelmed by hunger, he placed some pebbles in his mouth and found that they had turned to sugar which he could eat and continue thereafter to pray. This was seen as a special blessing from the Almighty on Farid. Yet another story talks of a time when he met some sugar traders travelling on camels. He asked them what they were carrying. Not wanting to tell the truth, lest they be made to share some of the sugar with him, they said that they were carrying salt. 'Then it will be salt,' he replied. On reaching their destination, the traders found that indeed their sugar had turned into salt. They travelled back to Farid, confessed their deceit and apologized, upon which he turned it all back into sugar.

The child was sent to Multan to pursue his studies, where his spiritual prowess was noticed by the visiting saint Bakhtiar Kaki who immediately accepted him as a 'mureed'. When he was sixteen, his mentor advised him to tour the Islamic countries and meet the leading mystics of the time. For the next eighteen years (1196–1214), Farid travelled to Ghazni, Baghdad, Afghanistan, Syria, Iran, Mecca, Medina, and to Jerusalem, recently opened to Sufis from all over the world by the conquest of Saladin. In Jerusalem he would fast and meditate, perhaps in his favourite way—hanging himself upside down for forty days in a dark room.

When Moinuddin and Kaki passed away in quick succession, Farid was presented with the latter's robe, turban, stick and wooden sandals. The mantle of the Chisti order fell on his shoulders. Finding that the intrigue-ridden atmosphere of Delhi did not suit his contemplative personality, he shifted to the quieter cantonment town of Hansi in Punjab. As his reputation grew, he left Hansi too for the remote town of Ajodhan which would soon become an important spiritual centre. His students studied, ate and slept in his humble home. Devoting themselves to spiritual development and contemplation, the master and students lived at subsistence levels, refusing to borrow money for food. On occasion they would circulate the 'zanbil', the basket made of palm leaves in which the townsfolk placed food for the dervishes who would divide among themselves whatever came as charity. All Farid had was a small rug on which he sat all day and with which he covered himself when asleep. He fasted all day, eating dried grapes with a glass of sherbet at the time of iftar, following it up with his evening meal of millet bread. Any provisions donated to the khanqah were distributed among the needy. The khanqah was open to wandering dervishes and many were those attracted to him, to pray and to study, to listen to his discourses, to hear his poetry in Persian, Arabic and Punjabi.

So Baba Farid lived on into his nineties, surrounded by his children and grandchildren and his favourite mureeds. Thousands of Sufis, supplicants, students and dervishes passed through his khanqah in Ajodhan. The mureed who would succeed him, and under whom the silsila would reach its pinnacle of glory and influence, was Nizamuddin Auliya, whose dargah in Delhi remains one of the holiest places in India, revered by Muslims and non-Muslims alike. Nizamuddin wrote of his spiritual master: 'The door to his hospice was never closed. Silver, food and blessings due to the kindness of the Almighty Creator—all were distributed from there to all corners. Yet no one came to the sheikh for material assistance since he himself possessed nothing. What a marvellous power! What a splendid life! To none of the sons of Adam had such grace been available.'

And this power, I cannot help thinking in the twilight, came all the way to Jerusalem and touched it so indelibly that I need to go searching for it after so many centuries.

4

A Ladder Forever on Golgotha

'"Takiya" and "zawiya", that's what Jerusalem was all about,' Sheikh Munir would reminisce to me late one Ramadan night, sitting in his courtyard, as the firecrackers burst near the Damascus Gate of the Old City.

'Takiya' in Turkish, 'zawiya' and 'ribat' in Arabic, 'khanqah' in Persian—all Sufi institutions built with charitable donations and differing only in degree; places of Sufi retreat; and home to the traveller, the poor, the mystic and the disciple. The leader of the order, the sheikh of the day, often lived inside the khanqah and organized celebrations of events related to the Prophet's life and the death anniversaries of venerated Sufi saints. Many khanqahs were meant especially for women and seven such, I find, were built in Aleppo alone in the twelfth century. Many were meant to venerate a saint or a hajji or to mark the place of a miracle. Some were built close to a small mosque or a religious school. But all based on the same principle, whether it was Farid's khanqah in faraway Ajodhan or the Zawiya al-Hindiya inside Herod's Gate, also known as Zawiya al-Faridiya or the Zawiyat al-Hunud, where he is said to have meditated for forty days, possibly in that underground room, accessible today only through a dark hole.

'All these are waqf properties... Most of the Old City was

waqf property,' Sheikh Munir continued. 'Old houses, coffee houses, public hamams, hospices, soup kitchens, were all waqf property for the welfare of the community.'

I do some more technical reading. The origins of the Islamic legal tradition of waqf go back to Caliph Omar, who had, at the advice of Prophet Mohammed, set up an endowment of some of his lands for the benefit of the needy. A waqf can be used for any charitable purpose, and it has always been considered more virtuous to make such an endowment in the holy city of Al-Quds. Under a waqf the property, which may be an orange grove, a mill, a fountain at the corner of a street, or a bakery producing 'mutabbaq' pastries or the humble 'ka'ek', becomes forever inalienable, a gift to God; and the income from it, after deducting the running costs, is tied up to the good of the community. 'Awqaf' (waqf in plural) are not limited to land and buildings alone: books and libraries, agricultural machinery, cattle and even cash can be awqaf. Solemnized before the sharia court of Jerusalem, the details of these awqaf are contained in the registries of the court, spanning centuries and now stored in trunks in several locations, chiefly on the Haram al-Sharif and in the nearby suburb of Abu Dis.

As I continue to search, I stumble across a paper called 'Sufism in Jerusalem under the Ottomans' written by one Zaki Hasan Nusseibeh. The coincidence seems too much; he must be connected to Sari Nusseibeh. On an impulse I pull out Sari's book *Once Upon a Country* and scan it chapter by chapter. And there, in the chapter tantazingly entitled 'The Key', in the last paragraph, is the reference to 'my cousin Zaki, the family historian...'

But such is the texture of the fascinating tales woven into the history of Jerusalem that I am not satisfied just with finding that reference. Transfixed, I read the whole chapter where Sari Nusseibeh traces the origins of his family's connections with Jerusalem through a 'beautiful mosaic of tales rooted in events both real and imagined…'

The story begins right with Prophet Mohammed. The tribal leaders who were the first to pledge their allegiance to him when he had been forced out of Mecca to Medina included a fierce woman warrior called Nusaybah, from whom the family gets its name.

A Nusseibeh forefather, Ubadah ibn al-Samit, was one of the companions of the second caliph, Omar, when he took Jerusalem in AD 638 after a long siege, entering the city on foot, wearing a camel-wool tunic. The humble caliph promised the Byzantine bishop of the city, Sephronius, that the people, property and holy sites of the city would be spared. So touched was the bishop that he handed the keys of the city and of the Holy Sepulchre to Omar. When the bishop led Omar to the Holy Sepulchre, the holiest of all Christian sites, the place of Christ's crucifixion and burial, Omar wisely refused to pray there, lest his followers turn the church into a mosque. He prayed nearby and as one would expect, there is the mosque of Omar right across the parvis of the Holy Sepulchre today.

Omar wanted to find the site of Solomon's Temple. Even though the Rock on the platform would not be associated with the miraculous night journey of Prophet Mohammed for another fifty years, Jerusalem had been the qibla towards which Muslims prayed in the first seventeen years of Islam. It was also the place where the ancient prophet Abraham came to sacrifice his son, where Solomon and David had prayed. Legend has it that the plateau had by then become a dungheap and Omar, accompanied by Sephronius, had to dig through the rubbish to climb on to the platform. Having reached the top, Omar set himself to having it cleaned up, much like Saladin would do five centuries later. The Al-Aqsa Mosque and the Dome of the Rock would be built on the platform before the century was over. Omar charged Ubadah and his clan, along with five other families, with keeping the Holy Rock clean. He also handed him the key to the Holy Sepulchre church.

The key to the Holy Sepulchre was a heavy burden. For centuries, a descendant of Nusaybah, now called Nusseibeh, would open the door of the holy church at the crack of dawn for the Christian pilgrims to file in, and lock up the church again at night. The family would be divested of the key for a short period during the Crusades, when the Franks took control of the city. But it would be restored to the Nusseibeh family once Saladin conquered the city and later agreed with Richard the Lionhearted to allow Christian pilgrims back into the city. However, about five hundred years ago, the family fell out with the Ottoman authorities and had to share its rights over the key with the Joudeh family. And that is how it remains to this day. A Joudeh brings the key to a Nusseibeh at four in the morning and the latter walks across to open the church. He puts the footlong skeleton key into the keyhole of a small door which forms part of the huge door. A priest from inside then hands him a ladder which allows the Nusseibeh to reach the main keyhole and open the gate. The present incumbent of the key takes his responsibilities seriously. He can often be seen near the entrance to the church, opening and closing a cupboard close to the ancient, heavy doors, handing out what must be a unique visiting card to curious pilgrims. It reads: 'Wajeeh Y. Nusseibeh, Custodian and Doorkeeper of the Church of the Holy Sepulchre.'

It's tradition on one hand and realpolitik on the other. The Holy Sepulchre houses various Christian denominations—Franciscans, Armenians, Copts, Ethiopians, Greek Orthodox, Syrians—and often they have more to fear from each other than from anybody without. They live in suspicious, uneasy coexistence, holding on fiercely to the rights of access and worship that they have in different parts of the holy site. And often they fight—disrupting services, stealing keys, making land-grabs on the important parts of the complex.

This too, then, is an aspect of Jerusalem—the key to the holiest

Christian site lies in the hands of Muslim families.

I also begin to understand what the Indian Franciscan priest, Father Jayaseelan—the only Indian priest to have lived in the Holy Sepulchre in two thousand years—had meant.

'On holy days, such as Good Friday, Easter Monday, Christmas Day, we have to be careful. There are hundreds of policemen inside the church,' he had said, in his understated, gentle manner, the perfect manner of the kind parish priest. I had made a mental note to ask him to take me in to the church on one of those days, when religious fervour is enmeshed with denominational rivalry.

It is Good Friday and pilgrims gather around the old olive trees of Gethsemane at the foot of the Mount of Olives where, two thousand years ago, Jesus sat, exhausted on the night of his arrest. I watch an Orthodox priest in his red habit pensively survey the church in the last bright light of the day. Then he gets up from the bench and walks away slowly.

I too turn away and take the steep lane to the Church of Mary Magdalene with its glistening onion domes. But it is shut; a small board says that the church opens only for two hours on Tuesdays and Thursdays. Some other visitors are more insistent than I can make myself be. They ring the bell and repeatedly speak into the door phone.

'We are from Rumania. Can we see the Church?'

But clearly the church is well and truly shut and I make my way across the Kidron valley or more precisely known here as the Valley of Jehoshaphat, and up the slope on the other side. There are graves all around; this part of the city is the necropolis of Jerusalem.

'Jerusalem is besieged by an army of the dead... I wander among the tombstones until I begin to think myself possessed,' wrote Herman Melville, the author of *Moby Dick*, in the middle of the nineteenth century.

It is no surprise, for the valley is associated with the Day of Judgement in the monotheistic religions. Here mankind will be brought to be judged at the time of the Apocalypse or 'Qayamat'; those buried here will be judged first; a bridge will appear from the Mount of Olives to the Haram al-Sharif across which the resurrected will walk; the Messiah will enter Jerusalem this way as he comes down the Mount of Olives—it will be his first coming; no—say others—it will be his second coming...

The Lions' Gate to the Old City is almost deserted. It is not yet time for the Muslim prayers and the Israeli guards standing at the porticoes to the Haram al-Sharif are at rest, lounging with their guns hanging low. A cold wind begins to chill the city as the sun goes down. Inevitably I look for coffee. This part of the Via Dolorosa is still empty—soon it will be filled with Christian pilgrims carrying crosses—and I walk slowly past the gates and doorways of the churches and shrines, the house of Mary, the prison of Jesus, under the famous arch known as the 'Ecce Homo' memorializing the words—'behold the man'—uttered by Pontius Pilate when he presented a scourged Jesus wearing a crown of thorns to a hostile crowd. It's possible that this was the site of the Herodian palace Antonia where Pilate held court but it is now believed that the arch itself was part of a structure built later by the Roman emperor Hadrian in the second century after Christ. Hadrian did other things too as he rebuilt the city as Aelia Capitolina, including building a temple to the goddess Venus over Christ's tomb and a temple to Jupiter on the site of the second Jewish temple.

The Al-Wad Street looks busy and interesting so I don't head for the café in the gardens of the Austrian Hospice; instead I settle down at a table set almost on the street by the Baasti Café ('since 1927—we have no branches'). Hot falafel, some chicken shish-kabab and a cardamom-laced coffee help me fight the sudden cold.

On the street everybody seems to be going somewhere. The

Jewish Passover has coincided with the Christian Holy Week and, within that week, the Orthodox and Catholic calendars have coincided to make it a special Good Friday. Orthodox Jews turned out in their shiny Shabbat best, with their circular 'shtreimels' on their heads, rush towards the Western Wall. Groups of Christian pilgrims begin to head down the Via Dolorosa towards the Church of the Holy Sepulchre to mark the crucifixion of Christ. Only the Muslims seem to be going about the ordinary business of the day: shopping, lounging in coffee shops. And a bunch of Israeli soldiers stand at the junction of the two streets, laughing and sharing a packet of potato wafers.

Reena Ninan, a tough and attractive reporter for Fox News, comes out of the Austrian Hospice lugging a tripod that is almost as high as her.

'We are going to do a live shoot,' she says and proceeds to set up her camera on the street. Even if she doesn't say a word, I muse, any audience would be happy to just witness the drama of the street, a view of this crossroad of three religions.

The Via Dolorosa is soon choked with people as one after the other the various Orthodox sects bring out the burial processions of Christ. Large crosses, flags, ornate robes, impressive beards and decorated cortèges pass by through the narrow lanes, all moving towards the Holy Sepulchre.

Suddenly the azan rises from some mosque. A very Jerusalem moment.

Father Jayaseelan is waiting for me in the crowded courtyard at the entrance to the church. I have never seen it so crowded and I am glad that he can guide me through the crowd. His brown Franciscan habit opens out a path for us.

The first sight of the crowd inside the church, the competing ceremonies of the various Christian sects, the several processions heading towards the entrance, seem to all make for a chaotic experience. The Syrians are singing outside the tomb of Christ, even while the Greek priests stand guard. The Syrian priests do not have the right to go inside. Even as the Father explains this to me, another group is approaching the tomb. And in their vanguard are two men, dressed in red tarbooshes, announcing the arrival of the group and clearing the way by banging their metallic staffs on the ancient stone floor. This method of traffic control dates back to the Ottoman years.

I follow Father Jay into the Franciscan vestry where the sword of the early Crusader Godfrey of Bouillon hangs near the door. The priests are getting ready to re-enact the crucifixion. Meanwhile, the swirling Armenian priests, led again by two staff-carrying heralds, have come to incense the Catholic chapel. Soon the Franciscan friars are ready, carrying a body of Christ which they will take to the rock of Golgotha at the other end of the Church. Everything seems to be happening at once.

But with Father Jay as guide, I can see patterns emerge out of the chaos. Centuries-old compromises have been worked out between the various denominations by the ruling powers in order to prevent clashes and conflict, not always successfully. While the Greek Orthodox Church gained predominance during the four centuries of Ottoman rule, it has not gone unchallenged. The main rivals are the Roman Catholics, here represented by the Franciscans or Latins. Several others too exist, often in more than one sect—the Armenians, the Syrians, the Copts, the Ethiopians, the Russians and the Rumanians.

The doctrine of status quo, first codified by the Ottoman rulers in 1853, has remained unchanged as there has never been any agreement on how to change it. Thus, existing rights to ownership, entry and worship are still in force, even if they don't always stand up to logic; even the right to sweep the dust off a particular place is determined and fiercely fought over. Emotions are most charged during the Easter weekend and the ruling powers of the day, be they the Ottomans of the past or the Israelis today, seem to have only one solution: they fill the church with policemen.

I follow Father Jay up the crowded steps to the chapel of Calvary where the crucifixion is to be enacted. Reaching the top of the steps, but not without severe resistance, we edge towards a corner to better watch the ceremony at close quarters. Father Jay tells me that half the chapel on top of Calvary belongs to the Catholics, the other half to the Greeks. The ceremony on Good Friday is conducted on both sides by the Catholics but the Orthodox seniors stand by quietly and watchfully.

A young priest steps up and pushes me back. 'This part of the chapel belongs to the Orthodox,' he says.

Father Jay steps in: 'Today it is permitted for everybody to be here.'

There is an increasingly heated exchange of words but the situation is quickly resolved by an Orthodox senior.

'Today we are welcoming the Catholics here,' he says.

The procession arrives; the body is nailed to the cross, then taken down and then carried away for anointment and burial. The poignant ceremony over, the Greek Orthodox take over their part of the chapel; I have seen the status quo work in practice under pressure.

As I leave that evening I glance up to the second storey of the church. Even in the gathering darkness I can make out a ladder placed against a window. It has been there for more than a hundred and fifty years; it is part of the status quo. And when it is worn down by the elements, it is replaced by a similar one.

When nothing is to be changed then truly, nothing is to be changed.

5

Coming Together under the Ottoman Seal

Another evening, a few days later. A cool breeze from my window, the Mediterranean a cloudy haze under a crayon sky, grey round clouds, a pink glow.

I return to the internet article by the historian Zaki Nusseibeh. A zawiya, he says, quoting from the *Encyclopaedia of the Orient*, is a shrine which is built around the residence or the grave of a holy man or woman, a 'wali' or a 'walya'. Zawiyas or 'zawiyat' are usually simple in their shape and interior, normally in order to reflect the ascetic lifestyle of the holy person—Sufi saint, hajji, teacher—they commemorate. The historian plunges into his sources; he has scoured the records of the sharia court in East Jerusalem and the books of the travellers who visited Ottoman Jerusalem. Men like Abed al-Ghani al-Nabulsi and Evliya Çelebi. Most of the Sufi khanqahs in Jerusalem were built under the Mamluks and by the time we come to Evliya Çelebi's account of the seventeenth century, there are seventy Sufi khanqahs in Jerusalem, belonging to various Sufi disciplines, or 'tariqas'. Where the Indian Hospice now stands, Zaki traces out, used to be the zawiya for the followers of al-Rifai tariqa, that was born in southern Iraq and reached Jerusalem through Syria. The founder of the tariqa, Ahmed al-Rifai, was credited with miraculous powers of healing but clearly unusual methods were employed: his followers would often stab themselves with knives in the ecstasy of meditation.

The fourteenth-century traveller Ibn Battuta too came across a centre of this tariqa where the mystics rolled in fire or extinguished it in their mouth to the rhythmic beating of drums and dancing during their zikr sessions. These are the howling dervishes, so called because of the nature of their meditation.

Some day I must try to trace out as many as possible of the zawiyat mentioned by al-Nabulsi and Çelebi, walk like they did through the labyrinthine lanes around the Haram al-Sharif.

But today, sifting through several articles and accounts, I want to keep my thoughts on the slimmest mention of the Indian Hospice, the Zawiya al-Hindiya or Zawiya al-Faridiya. Somehow, after the visit of Baba Farid to Jerusalem, the zawiya of the Rifai tariqa became the hospice for Indian pilgrims. Somewhere along the way, the Chisti order took over the 'chilla' of Sheikh Baba Farid (the word comes from 'chehel'—forty in Persian—the number of days that the saint is said to have meditated), purchasing the land in his name. Other accounts say that the authorities of the day had granted the original waqf, consisting of two rooms and a mosque, to the saint himself or to his followers, as recognition of his spiritual standing. One way or the other, as the years passed, Indian pilgrims purchased more land around the original allotment and it all became part of the waqf of the Zawiya al-Faridiya.

Or so I thought.

Nazeer's excitement the day he unearthed a long document from the Abu Dis archives was infectious. As we examined it, it was clear that the document that belonged to the Office of the Awqaf had painstakingly put together the record of the accretion of the present property. This document confirms that the original part of the Indian Hospice was on the Bani Zaid, or the little hillock inside Herod's Gate, its present-day position. It consisted of the mosque, the adjoining room and the area where the two old graves are. In the year 1824, the then sheikh of the hospice, Sheikh Ghulam Mohammed al-Lahori made out a case that the Indian Hospice that was in the 'maghribi' quarter of the city, that once lay in the vicinity of the Western Wall, was in a dilapidated condition and it would make sense if that property were exchanged for a property adjoining the premises at Bani Zaid. As a result of this exchange, he was able to add seven rooms, a courtyard and two water tanks. These, Nazeer points out, would be where the old rooms now stand at the far end of the courtyard, beyond the lemon and orange trees. The sheikh had to pay four hundred 'gersch' for this exchange, according to the same document.

A few years later, in 1846 to be exact, another sheikh of the hospice, Abdallah, added more property by buying the northern part, where the UNRWA clinic today stands for three hundred gersch.

So the whole picture changes. There were not one, but many Indian hospices in the old city of Jerusalem and it was only gradually that the hugely impressive seven thousand square metres of the present property was built up.

'Gersch?' I raise the question.

Nazeer points out a short note on the gersch, or more exactly, 'al-gersch al-assadi', contained in an anthology of Jerusalem's historical documents. The origin of the word may lie in the German 'groschen' but it entered the Turkish language as 'gerush'. This term has been used by Ottoman sultans in all their official documents and printed on their paper currency. The qualifier 'assadi' comes from the images of a lion ('assad') that it carries. The currency continued to be in use in Palestine till the end of the nineteenth century, each assadi gersch being equivalent to forty silver pieces.

The term 'assadi gersch', I am about to find out, occurs almost on every page of the documents Nazeer is carrying close to his chest, wrapped up in a sort of shiny brocade shawl.

'We are one of the few people who have managed to get ourselves registered in the last few decades,' Sheikh Munir is telling me when Nazeer walks into the little office at the entrance to the hospice. I have taken the chair that is placed just below the photographs of Nehru and Gandhi.

'Property is a very difficult matter in Jerusalem, and more so in East Jerusalem. If you have the records they are better than gold,' says Sheikh Munir as he watches Nazeer unwrap the bundle with the respect that one normally reserves for a holy book.

'You are one of the few people who has ever seen these files,' says Nazeer. He picks out one of the two files. It contains dozens of documents, in Ottoman Arabic, handwritten in black ink. They are all property documents going down centuries, signed and stamped by sheikhs and sharia judges long since passed into eternity. Haltingly we try to read a few, and then give up. It's enough to know that they are all there, safe. Someone has made an effort to preserve them, some simply by pasting the fragile fragments on thick paper.

'I think my father took them to the Rockefeller Museum long ago and they helped us protect these documents,' says Nazeer.

'No, it was my father, not I,' Sheikh Munir corrects him. 'He did it. I only saw these documents when I became the sheikh of the hospice, after my father's death. Before that it was difficult for me to get near them with all the problems that we had in the family. You know that I was not even staying for many years in the hospice because of the presence of my stepmother. So I had no hope of seeing these documents.'

This is the first I hear of a stepmother and family problems. But that will have to wait, I know.

And now he will not even countenance the thought of showing these documents to anyone with a view to further treatment. 'Now if anyone sees them, they will take them away. These are not good times.'

'And the second file?' I ask.

Nazeer smiles, holding the file fondly.

'This no one outside the family has ever seen before. This is a book written by my grandfather.'

I leaf through the manuscript. It is about three hundred pages in Sheikh Nazir Ansari's neat Urdu handwriting, mostly in black ink. On the cover, it says that these are notes and drafts about Palestine. Nazeer has tried to put the pages in some sort of order, but clearly this was very much a work in progress, perhaps a first draft of the old sheikh's book that was never actually completed. I wonder what it would reveal. An eyewitness account of Jerusalem for almost thirty years, years which saw the beginning of the Mandate, the struggle between Jews and Arabs, the Second World War, the creation of Israel and Jordan, the appearance of barbed wire and watchtowers across the heart of an ancient city. But the Urdu handwriting proves too complicated for novices and the secrets of that manuscript are soon returned respectfully to the warmth of the brocade shawl.

Perhaps it is now time to reach for his story.

6

The Khwaja from Ambheta

Sheikh Munir settles down in the comfortable drawing room with its long sofa and glowing electric rod heaters. Beyond the sheer curtains I can see the private courtyard with its water fountain, old olive tree and flower pots. This is the Travancore wing, where the family has lived since the bombs fell on the hospice in 1967. Here he is at ease, enough to begin telling me his story. We are still getting to know each other and he will be careful. In Jerusalem, especially in the Old City, people are slow to trust. So this will be the broad brush version.

But over the next year or more he will talk to me several times with varying degrees of enthusiasm and detail. Sometimes, just one incident will take an hour or two, punctuated by cups of tea; on other days he will dismiss an entire decade in a few sentences. Sometimes his voice will rise in excitement as the past comes alive for him, as brilliant as the sunshine in the courtyard. At other times, the memories, the nostalgia for a lost era or the spirits of the dear departed will draw the dusk around him in a sad caress and his voice will go down and the strong, reticent man will begin to choke and his eyes will go moist.

Often these stories would be interrupted all too quickly by other conversations, leading us away into one by-lane or the other—the ever-present politics of Jerusalem with its elements of treachery and deception, the cut and thrust of claim and counterclaim; or the adventures and tribulations of some member of the family and the ribbing that constantly went on among the siblings or Nazeer's good-humoured teasing of his wife Wafa.

But I had realized that there was no other way the story could be told. My only hope was that somewhere, in tranquil recollection, it would all come together.

'My father told us how he came to Jerusalem. He was living in India, in Saharanpur, in the village Ambheta near Saharanpur. They were four brothers and two sisters, of course from two mothers. My grandfather was a police inspector in Saharanpur. The first wife—this is what I heard—was of course Muslim, the second wife was Hindu. Two sons and one daughter from the Muslim wife, two sons and a daughter from the Hindu wife. My father's mother was of course Muslim.' When he spoke like this, his voice was even and calm, his eyes lowered, as if reading from some distant text inscribed within him.

'I don't think it happens often,' I interjected.

'No, it is unique. When he came here, my father left behind his Indian wife. Here he married one Palestinian and then an Indian.'

'Yes, you will find many things unique in this family,' Nazeer added, only half in jest.

I have childhood memories of Saharanpur, a yellow, hot, dusty town we used to pass on the way to Dehradun. Everything in that area smelt of sugar cane and overripe mangoes those days. We used to skirt around it, never enter it. Around it were shady dark green mango orchards, the trees laden with green fruit, the caretakers sleeping away the hot afternoon on charpoys, sticks in their hand, ready even in their sleep for the odd young boy who would not be able to resist the temptation of trying to knock down a mango or two. We would turn away before we reached the town, at the junction of Chutmalpur, a junction that seemed entirely to be made up of a couple of fuel stations, tyre puncture repair shops and some teashops with red ice-boxes prominently displayed, boxes full of Coca Cola, Fanta, Gold Spot... We would head off to the north, along a waterless riverbed, in which the villagers would be weaving rope, and rush for the Siwalik Hills which were already a low, green presence on the horizon.

It must have been an even smaller town then, fifty years before I began to travel past it, when Khwaja Nazir Ansari, the son of a police inspector, used to stay in one of the villages nearby. And for him, the move to Palestine from Saharanpur district must have been a very big one.

He left Saharanpur to finish his studies at the Aligarh Muslim University and then moved to Bombay, leaving his wife and two daughters in Saharanpur. It was at the time when the Indian Khilafat Movement was actively expressing support for the Ottoman Caliphate. Nazir Ansari too joined the Indian Muslim leaders of the time—the two brothers, Maulanas Muhammed and Shauqat Ali, who became leaders of the Khilafat Movement and went on to play an active role in shaping the structure of the post-Ottoman Muslim community, as well as other prominent men like Dr Mukhtar Ahmad Ansari and Hakim Ajmal Khan. It would be these leaders who, at the instance of a delegation sent by the mufti of Jerusalem, Hajj Amin al-Husseini, would depute Nazir Ansari to Jerusalem in 1924 to look after the Indian Hospice. The Ali brothers would part ways with the mufti later in life but at least on this one purpose, they worked together.

'Did you ever go back to Ambheta and meet the family?' I ask Sheikh Munir.

'Of course, I did. Even Nazeer went with me.'

He begins to do a quick mental calculation.

'It was then, in 1998, when we were invited to India by the government.'

Nazeer begins to add details: 'Our tour was arranged by the government. Our trip to Ambheta was also arranged by them. We went in a car, with a security officer with us.'

'And whom did you meet?'

'My uncle,' says Sheikh Munir. 'My father's brother, the youngest, Jamil Ansari. As I told you, there were four of them.'

'It was a great occasion,' adds Nazeer. 'The whole village came for the iftar with us.'

'It is not a village,' Sheikh Munir quickly counters his son.

'Of course it is a village,' insists Nazeer. 'Otherwise how could they all come to welcome us?'

I step in. 'A small town perhaps.'

'Yes, a small town at least,' says Sheikh Munir. 'And my aunt, she lived in the other town of Nakur, also a few miles from Saharanpur.'

Next day I look up the two places and find that indeed they are small towns. Not far from Saharanpur. Ambheta, the home of many Muslim families who converted to Islam during the Mughal period and also of others who came from waves of migration from the Arabian peninsula, Iran, Central Asia and Afghanistan. Among them were families using the name of Ansari, showing a link to Abu Ayyub al-Ansari of Medina, a supporter of the Prophet himself.

And Nakur has another link altogether—it was founded by the Pandav brother, Nakul.

'All of them knew about us,' Nazeer continues. They were carrying banners welcoming Sheikh Munir Ansari of Jerusalem. They had food with us, the entire village, sitting on the ground.'

'Not on the ground,' his father corrects him again. 'There were long wooden tables. And of course we saw the house. A very big house made of red brick. A porch with twin staircases going up. My uncle was living in one room. He showed me that the roof was leaking, the water from the rain was coming in.'

'Did you stay long?' I ask.

'No!' Nazeer is emphatic. 'We could not stay there. There was no electricity in the village. They brought a huge battery-operated light but I wanted to leave. I was sure we would be bitten by snakes at night. I asked the security officer to book us at a hotel in the nearest big city. So we stayed the night in Saharanpur.'

'Harram!' exclaims Jani. 'You went all the way and did not stay there? And you met the uncle only once?'

Sheikh Munir is quiet. Later I will understand his silence when he will tell me that once he had entertained a thought that some day he would give up his life in Jerusalem entirely and return to the village, or rather the small town where his father came from. Ambheta, near Saharanpur.

I never asked Sheikh Munir why the Muslim leaders of the Khilafat Movement picked his father to go and take over the Indian Hospice in Jerusalem. He, of course, had many qualifications to commend him. He was an active member of the movement. He also came from near Deoband, the home of the famous madrasa of Darul Uloom, and he had studied at Aligarh. These were the two centres of cultural and political activity of Indian Muslims after 1857, representing a social and political awakening, opposition to the British and support for Indian nationalism.

Or perhaps there is another reason, of which all the actors in this story were unaware, but which was always known somewhere in the cosmos. I find it in a lost page of the history of Saharanpur. The year is AD 1340 and Muhammad Tughlaq is campaigning in the northern 'doab'—the plain between the rivers Ganga and Yamuna—to crush the rebellion of the Shiwalik kings. While on the campaign he comes to hear of a holy man, a Sufi saint who lives on the banks of the Paondhoi river, in the dry bed of which the village women now weave ropes. He goes to see him and out of respect, orders that the place be known thereafter by the name of the saint. The name of the holy man was Shah Harun; the town, with due distortions, became Saharanpur. The saint belonged to the Sufi tariqa of the Chistis, the same order that had once been headed by the venerable Baba Farid. Perhaps there is a cosmic logic that a man from Saharanpur should come to look after the hospice where Baba Farid meditated.

Or perhaps there is no connection at all. But for some reason, the discovery sends a chill up my spine.

7

A Grand Surrender with Hospital Sheets

But the story is getting ahead of me. I need to rewind; I need to conjure up a picture, however sketchy, of the Jerusalem that Khwaja Nazir Ansari of Saharanpur had chosen to come to.

During the eighteenth century, Jerusalem was far from being a fabled centre of three religions. Rather it was a miserable, decaying town at the edge of the desert, not even a patch on cities like Baghdad, Damascus or Constantinople. The Ottoman Empire was in disarray. Its weak, dissolute sultans were unable to control effectively the governors, or pashas, who ruled different regions so they changed them frequently; the pashas, knowing they may be removed at any time, used their terms for quick self-enrichment. The travails of proper administration, the construction of new buildings or the restoration of monuments was not worth their while and hence far from their minds. A recalcitrant citizenry in turn resisted their rapacity and unfair taxation became difficult to enforce. The vacuum of leadership began to be filled by several leading families of Jerusalem—the Khalidis, the Husseinis, the Nashishibis... These families would become the city's nobility, producing its mayors and judges, scholars and wealthy worthies.

The plethora of waqf institutions of the city could not have escaped this downturn. Karen Armstrong in her *A History of Jerusalem* records that by mid-eighteenth century there were only thirty-five 'madaris' or seminaries left in the city and later these too would almost cease to exist. The awqaf dissolved in the face of the deepening impoverishment of the citizens; their assets were often leased out and even sold to non-Muslims.

The hard times did not gnaw only at institutions; they poisoned the dream of peaceful integration of Jerusalem's various religious communities too. Riots and clashes between different communities or even between different Christian denominations became increasingly frequent.

Fresh hope for the beleaguered city came in the mid-nineteenth century. A strong Ottoman commander, Muhammad Ali, took charge of Palestine and Syria and his son Ibrahim Pasha set up a secular administration and judicial system for Jerusalem. The main consequence of this separation of state and religion was a new lease of life for the dhimmis or the minorities—Christians and Jews at that time. Western Christian powers—Russia, Prussia, Britain, Austria—began to set up consulates and hospices in the city. The agenda was not only religious but clearly political; in fact, some have called this a 'peaceful Crusade'. Restoration of Christian sites started in real earnest. And not long after, Zionist colonies began to appear to protect Jewish interests. Money began to flow in from all directions into Jerusalem.

Arab Jerusalem also began to evolve its new identity, enriched by the members of the leading families. An active municipal council was formed with a mayor elected usually from one of these families. This council began to change the face of the Old City, cleaning streets, setting up parks, installing a sewage system. The construction of the houses of the notables began around this time outside the walls of the Old City, including the house that was to become the American Colony Hotel of today. By the 1870s there were fourteen new suburbs, a hotel near Jaffa Gate, a shopping arcade, museums, theatre, a post office and a telegraph system.

When the Great War broke out in 1914, Palestine began to writhe under the autocratic heel of the Turkish governor, Jamal Pasha. A rising Arab consciousness resented both the Turkish rule as well as the Zionist project; hope for survival with dignity lay in an Allied victory. The British fed these hopes: T.E. Lawrence gave assurances to Prince Feisal that, once the Ottomans were defeated, he would be given a unified Arab kingdom; British airplanes dropped leaflets containing the same promise from the skies over Palestine.

When tourists and visitors stream out of West Jerusalem's fancy hotels today and head towards the Old City, they usually enter it through Jaffa Gate, or Bab al-Khalil. It has a convenient road leading up to it that can take cabs and buses and a tourist office in its shadow. It also opens into the tourist-targeted Armenian shops, selling painted pottery, black-and-white photographs of the Old City, picture postcards, Bible leather sandals. Opposite them are the remains of a citadel called Tower of David. It has nothing to do with King David at all and is today the venue for a rather skewed historical sound and light show. In present times at least, the Jaffa Gate has established itself as the main entrance into the Old City. Pedestrians hook through its old opening, cars move in through the new one that was made to allow the procession of Kaiser Wilhelm II in 1898. Altogether it is a far gentler, far less shocking entrance than one through the traditional portal of Jerusalem—the Damascus Gate—which throws the visitor without warning straight into the bustling heart of the Muslim quarter.

The Armenian shopkeepers have stopped bothering me. They no longer even bother to sing a line or two of some Hindi song to attract me into their shops. They let me walk unhindered into the narrow alley below the Imperial hotel, a luxurious place a hundred years ago, a crumbling, disintegrating structure with wrought-iron balconies today, but not without charm. The alley leads to a little café and a bar. The coffee is good, the service unobtrusive and a Greek Orthodox priest with a glowing face, bushy beard, heavy dangling cross and robes of pure black can often be found seated at one of the tables to complete the picture.

It is through this Jaffa Gate that General Edward Allenby entered the city in 1917. He had marched with the 44th and 60th Divisions towards Jerusalem from the south and east, having been told by Prime Minister Lloyd George to conquer the city 'as a Christmas present' for the British people.

Much before he reached Jaffa Gate, and quite unknown to his intelligence officers, the last of the Turkish soldiers had already left the city in the pre-dawn darkness. The historian Ilan Pappé puts this turn of events into proper perspective: '...the last Muslim soldier had quit the city that had been under Muslim rule since Saladin had defeated the Crusaders.' The only surviving authority, the mayor Hussein Selim al-Husseini, put a couple of white sheets from the Italian hospital on a flagpole and walked out of Jaffa Gate with a ragtag delegation, mostly made up of the members of the Husseini family, in search of the British forces so that he could surrender the city into their hands. A few miles away they ran into two British scouts. Flabbergasted at being offered Jerusalem's keys, the two NCOs insisted that the ceremony await the arrival of an officer of His Majesty's service. A few hours later an officer duly arrived and obtained the mayor's letter of surrender on the back of a crumpled map! The moment that ended twelve hundred years of Muslim rule (but for the Crusader years) is captured in a photograph of confused sheikhs and officers.

The church bells rang out in welcome as Allenby dismounted from his horse and respectfully entered the city on foot, much like the austere Caliph Omar had done twelve centuries earlier. Accompanying him was T.E. Lawrence who had nothing to do with the battle, dressed out in borrowed uniform: 'The personal staff tricked me out in their spare clothes,' Lawrence wrote, 'till I looked like a major in the British Army. Dalmeny lent me red tabs, Evans his brass hat; so that I had the gauds of my appointment in the ceremony of the Jaffa Gate, which for me was the supreme moment of the war...'

When I pore over the old photographs of Allenby's arrival, it is possible to make out the Indian troops in his rank. Soon these smiling men with their fanned turbans would be photographed at many places in the Old City: a group of them posing outside Lions' Gate, a bugler poised against a clear sky, a guard checking a Greek Orthodox priest, three of them posing behind their gun, three or four others enjoying a light moment among the camels. These photographs would appear when I would be least expecting them—among the piles that lie in the souvenir shops of the Old City, in the shop of an old man who would entice me in with an offer of a glass of welcome lemonade on a hot day and then sell me an overpriced print, in the studio of an Armenian photographer who would tell me that this was the last day of the shop, the end of an era, and tomorrow he would retire forever.

Jerusalem remained under British military rule from 1917 to 1920. The military governor Lieutenant Colonel Ronald Storrs was a romantic aesthete, steeped in the classics, who devoted himself to restoring the city from the damage of war without destroying its ancient silhouette, composed of walls, minarets and turrets.

A pro-Jerusalem society was set up to look after the restoration of the religious sites. One of its recommendations—which thankfully holds to this day—is that all construction must be with the pale yellow brown Jerusalem stone. It is this stone that makes the city appear of one piece with the surrounding Judean Hills, with their timeless yellow rock outcrops amidst the thorn and the olives, and it is this stone from which a particularly warm rosy glow rises in the dying light of the sun. The British also completed a Herodian project for a water system for the city. They rid the city of locusts using stockpiles of poison gas and brought a sense of law, order and justice in which the middle class of Jerusalem as well as the elite families began to thrive. Tourists and pilgrims from several countries began to walk in the old streets again.

Arab–Jewish tensions were, however, building up. The Balfour Declaration, pledging the establishment in Palestine of a national home for the Jewish people had been leaked, arousing Arab suspicions. Realizing the perfidy of his own government, T.E. Lawrence returned all his medals. The rising communal tension erupted in the riots of 1920, particularly during the Nabi Musa procession. Anybody who is familiar even in passing with the history of Jerusalem would realize what an inflammable mixture that weekend was—the Muslim celebrations coincided with the Jewish Passover, the Orthodox Good Friday and the Good Friday on the Western church's Gregorian calendar. Jewish–Arab tensions provided the matchstick. There appears to have been another faint Indian connection: Ilan Pappé mentions that in the aftermath of those riots, Storrs stationed Indian Muslim troops in the Muslim quarter to check the women, believing that this would not cause offense. Many of the women, incidentally, were found with weapons. One day an Indian soldier accidentally shot a Palestinian woman near Jaffa Gate. The city shook as the rumour spread that the Orthodox patriarch had been assassinated and the Mandate authorities were hard put to control the consequences.

At that time the Palestinian elite was made up of representatives of the notable families but there was no clear leader. The British strengthened the institution of the mufti—a postion at the head of the Muslim social and religious authority to be held by a person by virtue of his command over religion and scripture. They picked the Jerusalem mufti of the dominant Hanafi school of Islam and made him the mufti of Palestine. The first incumbent was Kamil al-Husseini, the scion of the influential Husseini family, and largely an apolitical man. He was to be replaced after his death in 1921 by his more politically conscious and ambitious younger brother Hajj Amin al-Husseini with the backing of the first civilian British high commissioner, Sir Herbert Samuel. Hajj Amin was known to be an extreme Arab nationalist who had taken part in the 1920 riots. In fact Storrs had held him responsible for the Jaffa Gate riot and a court martial had sentenced him in abstentia to ten years imprisonment with hard labour. But ultimately he had been pardoned as the British manoeuvred between the promise of the Balfour Declaration and the surge of Palestinian nationalism.

Himself a scion of one of the notable families, Sari Nusseibeh provides a flavour of the Jerusalem hierarchy at that time:

> On top of the social pyramid sat the British governor, perched high on his white horse. He ruled from an administrative building on top of the 'Hill of Evil Counsel', where in New Testament times the Jewish high priest had his home. Then came the ornamentally dressed representatives of the various religious orders, led by Hajj Amin Husseini, the grand mufti of Jerusalem and the most important Muslim leader in the city, and the various Christian archbishops and bishops. Next were families like ours, still living off real or imagined past glories, whose children wore pressed suits and creased trousers and typically carried a volume of modern Arabic verse or *Robinson Crusoe* under their arms... Below the notables was the emerging class of urban professionals, mainly administrators, teachers and merchants. Finally,

> down on the bottom, were the hardworking peasants or fellahin, of the villages and countryside, proudly clad in the bright colour of their traditional dress. Rounding out the scene were Bedouin in long flowing desert djellabas, leading their camels through the streets, which now had a few private cars.

Hajj Amin, a striking-looking man with deep red hair and blue eyes, was young but had gathered a varied experience. Schooled in French and then tutored at the Al-Azhar University in Cairo, he had been a supporter of the Sharif of Mecca and later of his son Feisal who was trying to ensconce himself in Damascus. However, by the time he was appointed mufti, the dream of Palestine being a part of Southern Syria had evaporated; the Palestinians would now have to fight on their own against the promise of a Jewish Homeland and rising Zionism.

Hajj Amin's position was greatly strengthened when he also became the president of the newly formed Supreme Muslim Council in 1922 and took control of the powerful religious bodies, endowments and charities. This was to become his platform for opposing the Balfour Declaration. One of his first activities was to launch a construction and restoration programme on the Haram al-Sharif, the Noble Sanctuary housing the Dome of the Rock as well as the Al-Aqsa Mosque. The physical condition of these buildings was only one reason; the main impetus was political, given that the symbolism of these monuments was sufficient to revive Jerusalem's importance and restore its centrality in the Muslim and Arab world. In fact this activity would ultimately climax in the gold plating of the Dome. But this activity needed money and the mufti decided to launch a campaign to raise it. That was at least one of the reasons that the mufti deputed, in October 1923, a delegation to India, whose Muslim princes were among the richest in the world.

It was also an opportunity to meet and make common cause with the influential leaders of the All India Khilafat Committee, which had by now reached mass movement dimensions under the Ali brothers, on the many issues that faced the Islamic world at the demise of the Ottoman Empire.

At some time on that trip, the delegation from Jerusalem mentioned to the Indian Muslim leaders—the Ali brothers, Hakim Ajmal Khan, and Dr M.A. Ansari—that there was an Indian property in Jerusalem, an old Indian hospice in a state of disrepair. Should they not be sending a reliable and well-qualified Indian Muslim to look after it?

It was in response to this that the leaders turned to one of their activists in the Khilafat Movement, Khwaja Nazir Hasan Ansari of Ambheta, Saharanpur and asked him to go to Jerusalem.

8

Marriages in a Pile of Stones

'It was not as simple as that,' Sheikh Munir told me one day during one of our conversations. He had this way of mentioning an incident and then coming back to it much later to add new dimensions, layers, angles.

'My father met Maulana Muhammed Ali—already a senior Indian Muslim leader of the Khilafat Movement—one day, before he knew anything about the request from the Jerusalem delegation. He mentioned that he had had a strange dream. He had dreamt of a big place, a place with a tomb. He had visited that tomb and prayed. It was then that Muhammed Ali told him that his dream was going to come true, that they had received a request to send a good man to Jerusalem and they had thought of him.'

Shortly before his death, Sheikh Nazir Ansari would recall those days in a letter dated the first of November 1950: 'In 1924, the first Arab delegation arrived in India for collection of funds for the repair for [of] the Mosque of Omar. By the way they explained the very bad condition of the Indian hospice and that there was no responsible and [...] reliable Indian person to look after the hospice and they requested the Indian leaders at that time such as Maulana Mohamed Ali, Shauqat Ali, Dr Ansari and Hakim Ajmal Khan etc. to send a reliable man on their behalf to look after the pilgrims visiting the Holy Land, and the repairing of the hospice which is the only shelter for the Indians. On this request they selected me and sent me here with many introducing letters from them. On my arrival I was welcomed by local and government authorities, ever since I took charge of the hospice.'

When he arrived in Jerusalem in 1924, Nazir Hasan Ansari was welcomed by the Supreme Muslim Council and immediately proclaimed the sheikh of the Indian Hospice. Nazeer has found for me a document from the cavernous depths of the Abu Dis archives, its edges worn out as if by the heat of some flame. It is a notification from the Council to the director of the Office of the Awqaf, conveying the appointment, on 1 September 1924, of Sheikh Hasan Effendi Ansari al-Hindi as the sheikh of the Zawiya al-Hindiya in place of Hajj Ahmad, the sheikh so far. I wonder what Hajj Ahmad did to annoy the mufti to an extent that he manoeuvred the arrival of an Indian sheikh to take his place, but there are no answers to that question.

Sheikh Nazir was obviously not a man to let grass grow under his feet. The same day he proceeded to the hospice to take over the property from Hajj Ahmad. Another document dated the same day lists out an inventory of items that were handed over and taken over, with an eye for detail that would be the envy of any Indian bureaucrat. There is a list of seventy-nine items—pots and pans, carpets, chairs and tables—and it is duly stamped by the awqaf officials. He would devote the rest of his life to the building, repair and maintenance of the hospice. In two letters written just a year before his death, he recalls that parts of the hospice in 1924 were only 'a pile of stones. By the time and with hard work, I have succeeded to change the desert into a well organized place. This work was carried out with great efforts and good energy.' And at another place: 'From that time up to now I went to India several times for collecting funds and from time to time I made new buildings and repaired the hospice.'

He does not mention anything about planting trees in the hospice. For that I have to wait till a sunny afternoon in late February. A mild breeze ensures that I still wear a jacket and wisps of clouds throw a thin skein of flimsy white over a bright blue sky. As usual Sheikh Munir is standing at the head of the incline and greets me with a warm embrace. I cannot help remarking on the sense of absolute peace that prevails in the hospice.

'Yes, we are in the Holy Land, and though we don't see much peace around, we are fortunate in the hospice. The minute I walk into this gate I feel completely at peace,' he says.

I take in the moment with its bright sunlight, the fragrant cool breeze, the sounds of birds in the trees and agree with him wholeheartedly. Together we look up towards the tops of the fabulous tall trees, sturdy saru or cypress giants that line the path from the gate.

'These were planted by my father in the twenties,' says Sheikh Munir as we slowly walk back down the path. 'But I want to show you something.'

He points to an old tree whose trunk is half gone, but it still seems to rise towards the sky and is covered in green leaves. 'A rocket hit it in 1967 and finished it. It is dead but it still looks alive because other creepers have grown around the trunk and hidden the burnt shell. We had to fight to save the others too. During the intifada in the eighties, some youngsters were throwing stones at Israeli soldiers from near Herod's Gate. When they were chased by the soldiers they came and hid in the entrance of the hospice. The Unit Commander later came and told me that it had been decided to cut down all the trees as they were providing shelter to the miscreants and preventing the army from having a clear view. I absolutely refused. I told them—this is history, you cannot change the face of history. If you like you can control the entrance so that nobody comes in, but you cannot cut down the trees.'

So the saru trees planted by Sheikh Nazir in the twenties still stand tall, reaching out towards the brilliant blue sky.

'In India my father had the title of khwaja,' Sheikh Munir mentions as he examines the documents about his father's appointment as director of the Indian Hospice. 'That was an Indian title. His brother, my uncle, whom I met in Multan later—by that time there was a Pakistan and Multan was in that country—was called Khwaja Masud Hasan Ansari. Here, in Jerusalem, khwaja is used for non-Muslims and Christians. The titles for the Muslims are sheikh, hajji and so on. So he became a sheikh.'

His title was not the only thing that Nazir Hasan Ansari left behind in India. He also left behind a wife and two young daughters.

'Did you ever meet them?' I asked Sheikh Munir.

'Not his wife, the first one I mean. But I met the daughters; they were my half-sisters, Shakila and Naseema. And I met my uncle too, all of them during my first visit in 1950. By then India too had been partitioned, like Palestine, and they had moved to Pakistan. Even then, more than twenty-five years later, my uncle was blaming my father. He would say—"Munir, your father left his wife and daughters and never asked about them. And now you are coming, asking after them?"

'And my sisters, half-sisters, they treated me like my mother and sisters used to treat me. They made me sit on a chair and they would sit at my knees and serve me twenty-four hours. This is a dream for us, they would say, that this brother of ours has come from Jerusalem. Our father never asked about us and now this small boy, this Munir, has come all the way from Jerusalem...

'When my father came here, he was no longer a young man,' Sheikh Munir continued. 'He must have been about forty-five.'

'Did he know that he was coming here for life?'

A view of the hospice, probably during the early 1950s

Sheikh Nazir Ansari (centre) flanked on his right by Maulana Muhammad Ali of the Khilafat in traditional Arab dress, and by his brother Masud Ansari

Sheikh Nazir Ansari (front, extreme left) with Maulana Shaukat Ali (second from left) and the Grand Mufti Hajj al-Husseini (centre)

Munir with an Indian soldier during World War II

Sheikh Nazir Ansari with King Abdullah I of Jordan, circa 1948

A young Munir getting water from one of the wells on the Haram al-Sharif

Munir and Ikram on their wedding day

Mariam, alias Vilayat Sultan, (in white scarf) guiding Indian pilgrims around Jerusalem

Indian soldiers at Lions' Gate during World War I

Indian soldiers on security duty during the early Mandate years

An Indian soldier stands guard in the snow on the Haram al-Sharif

'I don't know but he stayed here twenty-seven years without ever mentioning that he would go back one day. Maybe,' he continued after a pause, 'it was because of his situation here. How to leave his family, where to leave his eleven children? He knew he was a foreigner and there was nobody here from his side of the family, no brother or sister.'

Eleven children! I make a mental note that I must try to know who they were, what became of them.

'How come he got married so quickly after coming here?'

Sheikh Munir smiles gently at my question.

'That is a long story. How he got married, first to my mother and then to Vilayat Sultan or Mariam… And, this very few people know, there was one more Indian wife in between. Nobody knows these stories, perhaps only I know them and my elder sister, Hind, she knew them. But she is no more.'

Then he goes silent, lost in thought or wondering how much of all this to share. Expectation seems to hang in the air and I find that it's not only I who is curious. Nazeer and his sisters have also gathered around and are quiet, not wanting to say anything lest they break the thread of their father's recollections. I am no longer sure how much of this they have heard before. Perhaps not everything or perhaps they haven't bothered to listen. We never bother to listen to the stories that our fathers and grandfathers have within their memories. And sometimes we leave it for too late.

'When my father started living in Jerusalem he was under pressure. You see, as a sheikh he could not be seen to be living like a bachelor. That would not be acceptable. He had to bring his wife from India or marry a local girl. So I think,' Sheikh Munir's smile turns mischievous, 'he found it easier to get married to an Arab woman, to taste a new kind of life. Of course it was an arranged marriage, arranged by none other than the Grand Mufti himself. The mufti did not want him to go back to India. He was afraid that if he went back even to get his wife, he may not come back at all. Or his wife may join him and not like it here and then force him to go back. So he hatched a plan to find a Palestinian girl for him and keep him in Jerusalem forever.

'The mufti's wife used to have a gathering every week at her residence where she would invite the prominent women in the city. They would talk, gossip and discuss various issues of the day. To this gathering she invited also my grandmother. Her name was Amina and my maternal grandfather's name was Hajj Hassan Najib. She was an illiterate woman, my grandmother, but you could open any page of the Quran and she would start reading it. She used to pray five times a day and later, many years later, she told me that this is one thing I should never neglect. She was my inspiration in many ways. She taught me how to accept the inevitable in life. She used to say, "*Ya molaklak la tolaklak ele elak elak wele lagerak moharam alek.*" (Much later, Nazer, the sheikh's eldest son, would send me a careful translation from Saudi Arabia of this old Jerusalem saying: 'You, the hesitant, do not be, what is meant for you, will be, what is not meant for you is forbidden to you.')

'They had only one child, a daughter. And very soon the mufti's wife suggested that they marry this daughter, who was to be my mother, to the sheikh of the Indian Hospice, recently arrived from India. She was very beautiful, my mother.'

'Yes, she was beautiful and blonde, I look like her,' Najam and Nourjahan say almost simultaneously.

'I remember her too,' adds Nazeer. 'She always told me not to carry my school bag always in one hand but to keep changing hands so that I would not get tired.'

'Those early years of my childhood, living with my father and mother here in this hospice were happy days. I remember some things. We used to live upstairs, in the part that was destroyed. First there were only Hind and I and then my younger sisters were born—Leyla, Amina and Fatima. There was a younger brother too, Nafez, but he died when he was only about a year old. So I was the only son, feted and taken care of. I remember going with my father to the Grand Mufti, who put me on his lap.'

'You were very fond of your father?'

'Yes, and despite the many things that happened later, I think he loved me too. Even in the difficult years when we were no longer living with him, he used to give me pocket money secretly. I learnt many things from him. He told me once that if you want to hit someone with a shoe, make sure you wrap it in silk. Yes, every time I went to him I would kiss his hand and he would bless me: "*Jeete raho beta.*" Even when we left the hospice—my mother and all of us—I used to go and visit him every day after school. Despite all that happened, yaani, he married another woman, I loved him, and I kept the good memories and the respect for my father.'

'But what went wrong? Why did you have to leave the hospice?'

'It was between them, between my mother and father. I used to tell my mother: it is your "naseeb". Yaani, this is chance, destiny. I suppose it was just the small things, small differences that come between a husband and wife. For instance, my father knew a lot of people and he would like to meet his friends in the evenings. From time to time he had to invite some people—Jewish, Christians, even the British. He had a very good situation with the Jews and the British. I remember that the director of the Hebrew University was his friend as was the governor of Jerusalem, a Britisher. He used to want my mother to join these gatherings. 'Um Munir', Munir's mother, he would call. But she would not come. I am a Muslim woman, she used to say, it is not right for me to come before strange men. Situations such as these would cause them to fight with each other. We used to tell her—this is his work, he has to meet these people; but it did not help.

'After thirteen years together, they separated. I was then ten years old. My mother and young sisters and I moved out of the hospice sometime in 1938, I think, and began to stay with my maternal grandmother. She was a talented seamstress and used to spend all the money she earned on us. Only later, my elder sister Hind came back to the hospice and started living with my father and his new wife. Those were difficult days.'

Of these difficult days he tells me another time. It's a day before Christmas in Jerusalem and I drive with the family to a restaurant for lunch. Nourjahan has chosen the restaurant and somewhat to the consternation of her father she also chooses to drive through the backlanes of East Jerusalem to reach there. It's in the Sheikh Jarrah area, not far from the American Colony Hotel, an area that is in the news almost daily as a venue of some protest, or of some demolition, or some other confrontation between Israelis and the Palestinians. The restaurant is dressed for Christmas—buntings, Santa Claus caps, stockings and decorative lights that are only faintly visible in the afternoon light of the courtyard where we sit on a long table. Behind the table is a door that seems permanently closed. It used to once lead into another house, I am told, but has been sealed off.

Sheikh Munir lets his daughters order the food. His mind is elsewhere, as if busy dragging back memories before they go over the edge into dark oblivion.

'It must have been 1938 when we moved out of the hospice and started living with my grandmother. We had to work hard to carry on our life and I was the only boy. My father used to give us only four Palestinian pounds although he lived like a maharaja in the zawiya. It was nothing, but he said that is all he could spare. Of course, as I told you, sometimes he would secretly give me some pocket money when I went to see him. Somehow we had to make ends meet. My mother would knead the flour at home and one of the children would carry it to the bakery to make bread for our meals. And I was responsible for getting water in cans from one of the dozen or so wells on the Haram near the Al-Aqsa Mosque.'

I didn't know it that Christmas Eve but one day I would walk with Nazeer down the Via Dolorosa, the route in the Old City on which the Passion of Christ is marked out in various stations. There he would point out a low arch over the road. The rooms in that arch were one of the places that young Munir and his sisters stayed in during those years of exile from the hospice. And I would also see, by and by, a photograph of the young Munir in sandals, standing near one of the wells on the Haram al-Sharif, preparing to carry water back for his family.

'We thought, of course, that we would go back to the hospice any day, that this was only a small problem between our parents that would be sorted out. But one day my mother came back from the mosque and she was crying. She had been seeing for some days another Indian lady, a dark-complexioned Indian lady praying in the mosque. But that day she met one of the workers of the hospice and asked him: "Who is this Indian lady?" He told her: "This is the sheikh's new wife." My mother was shattered.'

'This was the lady you call Mariam?'

'No, that is another story. This one was between my mother and Mariam. She lived only for a short while in the hospice, about eight months. We knew her as "Um Hani"—mother of Hani. She used to live downstairs and my father used to live upstairs. I think he wanted to keep it very private. But she didn't last very long.'

Sheikh Munir knows that his audience is hanging on every word and clearly he enjoys the situation.

'One day more pilgrims arrived to stay at the hospice. Among them was a lady from Peshawar, about thirty years old maybe. Her name was Vilayat Sultan. She was accompanied by some relatives—two brothers, one with a family and the other a bachelor. She was a very clever woman. She had come from Peshawar to Iran,

Iraq and then Jerusalem. She quickly assessed the situation at the hospice. Here was Sheikh Ansari from India, living upstairs while his wife lived downstairs. So clearly they were not too close to each other. In no time at all she was cooking some good Indian food and taking it up to Sheikh Sahib.

'Very soon the day of drama arrived. I remember going to the hospice after school, as I used to almost every day to meet my father. I found him with Um Hani and this new arrival, Vilayat Sultan. My sister Hind, who had by then moved back to live with my father, was also there. I asked her what was happening. She said that father wants to divorce Um Hani. And who is this other lady, I asked? Vilayat Sultan, my sister told me, she is the one behind this whole story. I was also witness to the divorce that then took place very soon.'

'It was that quick?'

'Yes, very quick. The next day we took a car for Um Hani from Jerusalem to Haifa and from there she was put on a ship to India. My father got married to Vilayat Sultan, later she would be popularly known as Haji Mariam. She took over his life, the hospice, everything. Unlike my mother, she was willing to be with him in all his activities. She would be ahead of him in meeting people. "Aaiye, you are welcome," she would say. She filled up all the gaps in his life. Khalas.'

'And your mother,' I tried to be gentle in my question. 'How did she take it?'

'What could she do? I remember, much like her earlier encounter with Um Hani, she ran into Vilayat Sultan too. We were walking in the Old City one day, my mother, grandmother, I and my three younger sisters. Here, near the Rockefeller Museum, we suddenly saw my father and his new wife and another Indian friend, face-to-face. My grandmother and mother accosted him: This is what you wanted, Sheikh Ansari? To leave your children, throw them out, and get married to others? And to her, they said: You succeeded in taking him away from us. And all of us, we cried.'

He sits sombrely amidst the Christmas buntings in the fading light of the winter afternoon, his voice choked with emotion. One of his daughters gets up and kisses him on the cheek, gently putting one arm around his shoulders. The other one gets up and with a paper napkin gently wipes the lipstick mark off his cheek.

But he is not yet finished.

'People have often wondered why I did not marry other women like my father. Because I did not want my children to suffer like I and my sisters did. Life is more than just marriage, food and bed. Today I can walk with my head held high. I am Kabirna, the Elder, to many. I am respected because I have done all I could for my wife, my five children, my grandchildren.'

A grey afternoon has descended outside; it is almost four o'clock. The restaurant has no Arabic coffee. Only espresso and cappuccino; it is after all an Italian restaurant. 'But you must also look at the surroundings, see where you are; you must have Arabic coffee...' the restaurant manager is severely admonished by Sheikh Munir as he steps quickly into the present. We say our farewells. I need to catch a nap after the long conversation and heavy food before I try to get to Bethlehem and find a way to be present at the midnight mass at the Church of Nativity, the birthplace of Jesus Christ.

9

'Allah Will Provide the Means'

While the high politics of the Mandate era was being played out, while Sheikh Nazir Ansari abandoned one wife to marry another, and then yet another, the daily business of the Indian Hospice did not stop. Gradually, the 'pile of stones' that Sheikh Nazir had found on his arrival there began to take shape with the assistance of the rich Muslim princes of India.

The Palestine Post of October 1934 records the visit of the nawab of Rampur, Muhammad Raza Ali Khan, to Jerusalem. Accompanied by his begum and sundry valets, ADCs, a staff surgeon, a nursing sister and other household members, the nawab housed himself at that newly built icon of Jewish Jerusalem, the King David Hotel. He could well afford to—*The Palestine Post* noted when reporting the visit that he was one of the richest princes in India, whose state library was famous for its ornamental manuscripts and magnificent collection of portraits from the sixteenth to the eighteenth centuries.

On 21 October, the nawab accompanied by his entourage visited the Nabi Musa shrine outside the city, Jericho, the Dead Sea and then headed towards Herod's Gate and stepped inside the Indian zawiya to be warmly welcomed by members of the Palestine–Indian Association, headed by Sheikh Nazir Ansari. The nawab and his entourage were given a full tour of the hospice and briefed on its historical significance. Sheikh Ansari, no doubt, explained to them the plans that he had for repairing and expanding the premises. The nawab's help was sought for the fulfilment of these plans. According to the *Post*, 'he readily agreed, undertaking to pay for the rebuilding of four rooms to be named "Raza Manzil".'

An announcement placed the amount of grant at five hundred Palestinian pounds but, for some unfathomable reason, the first instalment that he issued was for an amount of 223.50 pounds.

Nazeer has unearthed for me two documents that show how the work was done. First in 1934 the director wrote to the engineer in charge at the Awqaf headquarters, saying that they had received money from the nawab of Rampur and intended to add a building. A drawing of the proposed building was attached and clearance was requested at the earliest. And in 1935 the contract for the job was awarded—not to the cheapest applicant but to the best contractor.

Today the Raza Manzil contains the visitors' room of the hospice. On one side of the room stands Sheikh Nazir Ansari's ornate writing desk on which a visitor's book is placed. Sheikh Munir or Nazeer never fail to have the name, address and impressions of every important visitor to the hospice recorded in these books. On the walls of the room are framed photographs, photographs of the early hospice at the beginning of the twentieth century and others which document the visits of many dignitaries to the institution in more recent years. Similarly the Usman Manzil, through which one enters the hospice today and which houses its working office, was built with funds received from the Nizam of Hyderabad.

Clearly, by the thirties, Sheikh Nazir had become a prominent notable of the community. Heading the Palestine–Indian Association and being an active member of the Supreme Muslim Council on the Haram must have added to his stature, as also his close association first with the Grand Mufti himself as well as the leaders of the All Indian Khilafat Committee. In the small personal cabinet of the director of the Indian Hospice, the one with the chequerboard floor of black and white, sharing the wall with photos of Mahatma Gandhi and Jawaharlal Nehru are those that show Sheikh Nazir with the two Ali brothers. All this enabled him to act almost as an honorary consul of India. Several letters can be found in the records of the hospice whereby he recommended travellers for entry to other countries, standing guarantee for their reputation and good conduct. In fact, in a minor way, he was following in the tradition of consuls of several European countries—French, German, British, Russian and Austrian—who had wielded considerable influence, and enjoyed demigod status in Jerusalem during the Ottoman Empire.

'Whenever he went out he was accompanied by the ten or fifteen hajjis who stayed at the hospice. They were like his bodyguards. He was a big man in Jerusalem,' recalls Sheikh Munir with a faint touch of pride.

An attestation dated 17 August 1935 signed by one Syed A. Rafique, MA Cantab, Barrister-at-Law with an address of Star of India, Calcutta, says it all:

> The Indian Zawai [sic] under the able guidance of Maulavi Nazir Hassan Ansari, is a standing testimony of the fact that great works for the betterment of the Muslim community are nearly always founded on the personal sacrifice of an individual. In this case it happens to be a man of a distinguished family who renounced the ease of his own home and undertook a voluntary role to serve the Muslim community. The Zawia from being merely a name is now a living institution giving its services without asking any questions to whomsoever of the Indian Motherland, who cares to knock at its door. Rich and poor here are treated alike and no effort is spared by Mr. Ansari in making his guests feel at ease and at home...

And the pilgrims kept coming. Years later, in a letter dated 11 October 1949, Sheikh Nazir would write: 'In 1939 when the war broke out, the pilgrims and visitors stopped coming to Jerusalem Palestine from India. Before that from 1924 to 1939 average 2000 (two thousand) pilgrims and visitors were visiting Jerusalem and staying in Indian Hospice.' In fact an earlier document—the register of foreigners in institutions in Jerusalem in 1883—notes the presence of 1530 Muslims, 'dervishes and others' in the Indian Hospice in the Bab Hutta quarter which compared favourably with 487 North African dervishes and pilgrims and a later 1905 entry of ninety-four Afghan and Uzbek dervishes and pilgrims.

To take care of the pilgrims, the sheikh received ten Palestinian pounds per month from the Special Fund of the Ottoman Empire for running charities. This payment would continue till the end of the British Mandate in 1948 to be replaced by a payment of one pound from the same fund but paid through the waqf department of Jerusalem. In addition there was the donation of four and half kilos of bread daily from the Khaski Sultan Takiya. This was replaced later by a payment in cash. In an old document that details the disbursements to various institutions from the Turkish financial allocation in the year AH 1205 (AD 1790), it is mentioned that the amount disbursed 'from the waqf of the Turkhan Bek (may his soul rest in peace) for the Indian Hospice of Sheikh Farid Shakarganj is 30 *assadi gersch*.' Somehow the hospice was able to make ends meet with these resources, plus, of course, the contributions that the pilgrims would sometimes make.

I probe the sheikh's memories about the pilgrims.

'I don't remember from the time of my father,' he says. 'But I remember from after 1948... They would come from India to Basra by boat. Then from there to Baghdad and then to Jerusalem by buses. They would be on their way to the Hejaz, to Mecca and

Medina for the hajj. They would bring everything with them—children, folding beds, bedrolls, tents, chawal, dal, even stoves and kerosene oil, all the way from India. Five or six of them—a family—would take one room and one corner of the room would become a kitchen. In the courtyard, here where we enter the hospice, women would be washing clothes like dhobis. Somebody would be speaking in Punjabi, some in Bengali... This place would become like a small village.' Then he lapses into Urdu—*'Idhar khana pakana, udhar kapde dhona...'*

'They would continue on their hajj from here or come here on the way back. By bus. Earlier on, my grandmother used to tell me, they travelled from here to Mecca by camel. It used to take them about two months. They would hang their folding beds on the sides of the camel from the howdah. But sometimes we got richer pilgrims, say from South Africa. They did not bring their beds or food and these had to be provided for them.'

Searching through the snippets of *The Palestine Post* that Nazeer has now been assiduously putting in plastic sleeves, I come across a story titled 'On the Road to Mecca'. It is dated 13 February 1935, a day when, according to the same paper the Meteorological Station in Jerusalem (situated, as the report says, 757 metres above sea level) recorded a temperature of 16 degrees at 8.00 a.m. and a moderate south to south-westerly wind with a whimsical prediction of 'perhaps light showers later'.

> A bus load of British subjects on their way to Mecca stopped outside the General Post Office. They were in white robes, some with white turbans, others with brown headgear. They numbered about twenty men and women. Most of them hail from the regions north of Bombay, and they had traveled by sea from Karachi to Basra, thence overland to Baghdad, and Jerusalem.

The simple story of their months long journey was told me by the leader, a tall hajji with a shred of green peeping from beneath his turban. He spoke a few words of English as we stood in a queue inside the post office buying stamps. He had just chartered the bus to take them to Amman, he said. They had finished their pilgrimage in Jerusalem, and after a stay at the Indian Zawia, they were off for the holy cities of Hedjaz.

'My friends have been saving for years to come here,' he pointed to them seated patiently in the bus flanked by a crowd of curious sightseers. 'They are peasants and shopkeepers, they are poor but they are of the true faith, I myself am a hajji of Mecca.'

I told their leader that they might find it difficult to leave Amman on their way southwards because of chaotic communications.

'Allah will provide the means,' he said resignedly. 'We have been a long time on our way and we have seen many cities and many things. It is Allah's will that we should reach Mecca in good time.'

One distinguished visitor to the hospice in 1937 was the sultan of Kano, a province of northern Nigeria, on his way back from Mecca. *The Palestine Post* of 28 March that year reported that the sultan was received at the railway station by the mufti and the important sheikhs of the Supreme Muslim Council and proceeded to stay along with four of his ministers and his son at the Indian Hospice. The *Post* proceeded to explain that Kano is a province of over two million inhabitants, situated 'roughly between the Niger and the Lake Chad'.

Sheikh Munir has only a faint memory of that visit. 'I was only as old as Faris,' he says, pointing towards Nazeer's son, who is trying to climb the olive tree in the courtyard.

There is another intriguing entry in *The Palestine Post* of the same year. It is titled 'Sultan of Bahara in Jerusalem'. Sultan Tahir Said al-Din is said to have come from India with one hundred and fifty of his followers. In India he is supposed to have two million Muslim adherents. I can only conclude that the reference is to Sultan Taher Saifuddin of the Bohra community. 'At the Jerusalem station,' the report continues, 'he was welcomed by the Mufti and other Sheikhs of the Supreme Moslem Council and a number of Arab notables including Ragheb Bey Nashashibi. A troop of Arab boy scouts paraded in his honour and there were two bands from Moslem institutions...' The sultan was reputed to be 'a man of great wealth' who had made 'substantial contributions to the religious and political funds of the Arabs of this country', which perhaps explains the warm welcome at the station by representatives of both the rival factions of the Palestinians. There is no mention of a visit by the Bohra sultan to the Indian Hospice but given his Indian background and the likely presence of Sheikh Nazir Ansari among the members of the Supreme Muslim Council in the welcoming party, it is likely that such a visit took place. There is nothing in the hospice that marks any contribution though.

Weeks after I have read about it, I get to asking Sheikh Munir what he remembers of the Bohra sultan's visit. We are sitting in the veranda of his house in Jericho, a house where he spends several days each winter. It's a large comfortable house, low and flat, the kind of house that all hot cities have. And Jericho, far below sea level and within sight of the turquoise blue Dead Sea, is nothing if not hot in the summer with the temperatures going up to 55 degrees. But the day is a lovely sunny day in late December and the sheikh, immaculate in a tweed jacket, is in a good mood. He proudly shows me around the house and the garden with trees loaded with clementines and pampelmoes.

'We built it in the early seventies,' he recounts. 'My three elder children—Nazer, Najam and Nazeer—they were very young then. They used to help with building the house, painting walls, putting bricks. This swimming pool was one of the first to be built in Jericho but it needs repairs now.'

I can see that; the side walls of the pool have begun to crumble. 'During the first intifada we could not come to look after the house. Our fruit trees were burnt and people began to camp in this house. I suppose they were not sure who this house belonged to, what kind of people we are. Now they all know us here; we are known as Ansari al-Hindi.'

'There was no way of coming by the road to Jericho during the intifada,' Nazeer adds. 'My father and I came walking through Wadi Qelt from Jerusalem to claim our house.'

I glance towards the stony hills beyond which, several miles beyond, lies Jerusalem. At the foot of these hills lies the site of the old city of Jericho. It is a somewhat unkempt archaeological site where layers of settlements from the ancient times are visible, including a tower which has been dated as ten thousand years old. And clinging to the rock face high above on the Mount of Temptation is a thirteenth-century Greek Orthodox monastery, built around a cave where Christ is believed to have fasted for a full forty days and resisted the temptations put in his way by the Devil. This is the source of the saying that man does not live by bread alone.

We come back to the sheikh's memories of the sultan of the Bohras.

'I met him during my visit to India in 1956. I had gone with my wife and my son Nazer, who was then three years old. We first took a boat to Karachi. Then I went to see my half-sisters in Bahawalpur and my uncle in Multan. After that we went by road into India, from Lahore to Amritsar.'

'And to Ambheta,' adds his wife, from the far end of the table.

'You went to Ambheta?' the sheikh turns to his wife.

'Of course,' she says, 'you have forgotten.'

He shrugs gently. He seems reconciled to the fact that memory has begun to play tricks. But he carries on.

'We went to Bombay and to the house of the sultan. He had a very formal court, with people standing in attendance around him. He met me very nicely and asked about my father. Perhaps he did come to the hospice during his visit to Jerusalem after all and had met my father. I told him that my father had passed away some years earlier and that I was now the director of the hospice. Then he called one of his attendants and whispered something. The attendant took me to one side and told me to come back in two days. This was a problem for me. We were supposed to leave the next day, our berths were booked on the ship for Basra. But now we could not leave. Finally, we changed our tickets and came back after two days. I was given a gift.'

'Twenty kilos of gold?' Nazeer asks him playfully.

'Gold? He gave me a shawl! But it was a very fine shawl.'

'What did you do with the shawl?' I asked him.

'I came and gave it to Mariam.'

'Not to your own mother?'

'No, she was upset with me about it but still I gave it to Mariam.'

He falls silent. In the distance I can see the cable car going up the brown rock face. It will stop with a little jerk and pilgrims and tourists will get off, walk past several little cafés and climb the narrow path towards the Cave of Temptation, not quite able to believe that they are actually there.

10

'You Are a Man Now'

Much was also happening meanwhile outside the Indian Hospice.

On the surface, the early years of the British mandate were peaceful under the first two high commissioners, Sir Herbert Samuel and Lord Plumer. The Zionist community, largely homogeneous in nature, consisting of Jews from East Europe, moved with solidarity towards constructing the infrastructure of a state. An underground army (Haganah), a parliament of representatives from the kibbutzim and the trade unions (Histraduth), taxation, legal and financial institutions as well as health and educational systems, including a university on Mount Scopus, came into being. The Arabs, by contrast, were weakened by factionalism and the fierce rivalry between the Grand Mufti who belonged to the Husseini family and the Nashishibi clan. They differed on tactics as to how to stop the Zionist machinery and how to work with the British regime.

The mufti in particular was hopeful that pan-Arabism would help the Palestinians resist Zionism. He was also very active in the larger Islamic politics of the post-Ottoman world in which various personalities and entities, ranging from the sharifs of Mecca, King Feisal of Baghdad and King Fouad of Egypt vied with each other to inherit the Caliphate and the leadership of the umma. This interaction kept him in close touch with the Indian Khilafat Movement, one of the most influential forces in Islamic politics of that era and the Ali brothers. When Muhammad Ali died in 1931, the mufti wired his brother Shauqat Ali offering burial in Jerusalem in the vaulted alcoves on the Haram, a few yards away from the venerated Dome of the Rock. The funeral served the mufti's purpose of encouraging Indian Muslims to look towards Jerusalem as a seat of their religion, equal to Mecca and Medina: also, after 1931, the numbers of visitors from India increased to hundreds. The mufti's association with Indians, in particular the Ali brothers, was born out of his need for financial and political support; they in turn needed support in the Arab world for their aim of restoring the Caliphate and fighting imperialism. But during the Jerusalem Muslim conference of the same year, the mufti seems to have fallen out with Shauqat Ali who led a small dissident faction, with the two luminaries vying for the presidency of the conference.

In 1929, when our Sheikh Munir was all of one year old, unprecedented violence broke out in Jerusalem between Arabs and Jews over prayer arrangements at the Western Wall. During the Ottoman years, the Jews had to obtain permission from Muslim authorities to visit the wall but under the Mandatory government they were allowed to increase their presence gradually. There were attempts to purchase the site but these were thwarted by the Palestinian leaders. Increased Jewish presence and the bringing of chairs and benches as well as religious artefacts raised fears among the Arabs of a Jewish takeover of the Haram, believed to be the site of both the Solomon and the Herodian Temple. The sound of the Jewish shofar was countered by loud zikr from a neighbouring Sufi khanqah, the muezzin timed his call for prayer with the Jewish prayer services and what had been a cul-de-sac was turned into a thoroughfare through which Arabs could lead their animals, much to the anger of the Orthodox Jews. Confrontation and clashes became inevitable. Finally, when the Western Wall riots broke out, several hundreds died on both sides; historians differ on exact numbers. It was clear that the extremist factions on both sides were beginning to take control and the British were inevitably giving up attempts to achieve a solution. In desperation, they poured in more soldiers.

Tensions erupted in full again in 1935, led not by the mufti this time but by a village cleric, Sheikh Qassam, and fuelled not so much by high politics but by the pauperization of rural Palestine. This was followed by a general strike including large nationwide demonstrations against the Mandate in 1936 called by the Arab Higher Committee under the leadership of the mufti. A full-scale violent rebellion was to follow in 1937. The Mandate government reacted sharply to the assassination of the acting British district commissioner of the Galilee and put the blame on the members of the Arab Higher Committee and exiled them. The mufti took sanctuary in the Haram al-Sharif before escaping arrest by sliding down a rope thrown over the walls and left for Beirut, dressed as a woman. In the following years he would use every opportunity to ally himself with anti-British forces and would even end up damaging the Palestinian cause by actually allying himself with Hitler.

Sheikh Munir has a memory from those days, or a few years later: that of the Mandate Police, which seems symbolic of the ambiguous situation that existed. 'I remember,' he says, 'that they used to send out two policemen to patrol the streets at night. One would be Jewish and the other Arab and both would have the insignia PP—Palestine Police—on their caps. Only that their caps would be different. The Arab would wear what we in India would call a 'kulla', with a hard centre and the Jew would wear a khaki peaked cap.'

Another incident of those days that he relates shows that somewhere the Grand Mufti, and the man he had been instrumental in bringing from India to Jerusalem, Sheikh Nazir, had parted ways. The incident took place at a time when the mufti had launched the general strike against the British, building on the rural revolt of Sheikh Qassam. By that time, Sheikh Nazir of the hospice had begun to side with the rival Nashishibi family.

'We were already staying outside the hospice then, separated from my father who had by then married Mariam. One day I came to the hospice to look for him and did not find him in the usual room upstairs. Nor did I find Mariam. I asked the hajjis, the dervishes who used to stay in the hospice, but they too seemed unaware of their whereabouts. For the next three days I came every day and still could not find any trace of my father.

'I was completely distraught. In tears, I went to the house of Fakhri Nashishibi in Sheikh Jarrah. There were two uniformed guards standing outside the house. I told them that I was the son of Sheikh Nazir Ansari of the Indian zawiya and wanted to meet Fakhri Nashishibi. He was an important man then, a major leader who was supporting the partition plan of the British. I was finally allowed to go in. The big man met me very nicely. He hugged me and made me sit down. I was offered sweets and fruits. Then he said: 'You are a man now. I will tell you why your father had to be sent away.' He told me that a man had been caught at the border between Jordan and Syria. In a paper hidden under a bandage on his arm were found a few names, these were the names of people the mufti wanted assassinated. My father's name was among them. That is why Fakhri and his people had made him and Mariam leave the place within twenty-four hours. They were already on a boat sailing to India from Haifa. That was it. There was nothing I could do. My father remained in India for six months or so. Then things changed. The mufti escaped from Palestine, the Second World War started. My father and Mariam returned to the hospice and soon the place was turned into a leave camp for Indian soldiers fighting in the area for the British. And Fakhri Nashishibi himself fell to assassins in 1941 in Baghdad.'

I turn to the snippets from *The Palestine Post* of those years that Nazeer's enthusiasm has unearthed. A report of 8 May 1933 announces that on 5 May, two Arab delegations left Jerusalem, one for India and the other for Iraq. The delegation that went to India was led by the mufti himself and had as its secretary, Sheikh Nazir Ansari. The report continues: 'An announcement was made by the Moslem Supreme Council to the effect that the delegation has no other aim than to collect funds for the proposed Moslem University of Jerusalem. This displeases "Falastin" which is anxious that the delegates should imitate the Zionist funds for buying land and settling people thereon...'

Another article in the same paper, dated 26 December of the same year probed the real purpose of the mufti's visit. 'The object of the visit was ostensibly to raise money for a proposed Moslem University in Jerusalem, somewhat less ostensibly to raise money for land purchase to defeat certain Jewish land redemption schemes, but actually the purpose of the Mufti's mission was [...] the fanning of the anti-British spark into a flame, using Palestine as a pretext for setting Moslem feeling ablaze.'

In the event, the visit did not succeed either in raising an anti-British sentiment nor in raising funds. Meanwhile, according to another snippet in *The Palestine Post*, the Palestinian Indian Association met at the Indian Hospice and sent a resolution to it seems just about every British authority around—the High Commissioner, the Palestine Government, Force Headquarters and the District Commissioners—'expressing loyalty to and support for the British Empire in this hour.' The resolution was signed by, among others, Nazir Hasan Ansari, Treasurer.

Yet another report from July 1934 throws more light on the murky politics afoot. It talks of a visit to Palestine and several other countries by the president of the Indian Khilafat Committee, Sayed Murthada Bahadur and Maulana Shauqat Ali. While the touted purpose of the visit was to discuss the Palestine Arab problem, the real purpose was 'the election by Moslems the world over of the Nizam of Hyderabad as Caliph of Islam.' The nizam 'is said to be the richest man in the world. His jewel collection is said to be the finest one extant. His subjects number 11 million Hindus and 1¼ million Muslims. His two sons a few years ago married the two daughters of ex-Sultan Abdul Medjid, the former Caliph, who was deposed by Mustapha Kemal Pasha from his throne in 1924 and later resigned the Caliphate.' Naturally, the mufti was opposed to such a move and equally naturally, the rival Nashishibi faction was sympathetic.

The sheikh from Saharanpur was holding up the Indian flag in the midst of very murky waters indeed.

II

The Diary of an Oud Player

Sheikh Munir is waiting to greet me in the small garden outside his house. On Fridays, he usually sits down to lunch at two after his return from the mosque, with those members of the family who happen to be around. It's well past that hour and I am conscious that I have delayed him but he brushes aside my excuses and invites me to the full table.

Najam, dressed in summery white, has excelled herself. Chicken breasts stuffed with rice, pasta, tabbouleh, hummus and falafel to which Wafa has added a sort of shrimp biryani. There are delicious Jericho melons and watermelons to follow.

The lateness of the hour is brought home again: before we have finished, the call for the prayer of Asr, the third prayer of the day, begins to rise in the sky. It is rising from somewhere very close and Sheikh Munir takes me to the kitchen window. Drawing my eyes back from the Mount of Olives glistening in the distance, he points to a small mosque that is so close to the hospice that the loudspeakers for the call for prayer have been put up on hospice land itself. But here too politics lurks not far below the surface. Once or twice, the Jewish settlers who have taken up a house across the lane have cut the wires of the loudspeakers. The call for prayer was too loud for them.

In the garden there are sweets—the gulab jamuns I have carried and their close Arabic cousin, the zalabiye—and many cups of Arabic coffee. Nazeer has pulled out a box of old photographs which Sheikh Munir says he hasn't seen since 1967, when so much happened at the hospice. Most of the photos were taken with the box camera that a young Munir, fascinated with photography, had bought for half a Palestinian pound in 1936.

The fountain is gurgling; a cat takes a quick jump and then sits motionless among the fabulous geraniums. A slight breeze, cool and fragrant, rustles itself to motion under the olive tree. The sheikh's grandson Faris begins to climb the olive branches.

The afternoon is dying, gently; it is time for memory to speak.

'The Usman Manzil, the building that we enter the hospice from and where we have the small office, was built in 1936, when my father collected donations for it from the nizam of Hyderabad. Of course there was an old building there before it. And there were seven wells inside the hospice. These wells were very important in any Jerusalem house. One of them used to have very cold water. They can work even now if we repair them. There were many wells on the Haram al-Sharif—that water was good for drinking. I used to go and bring buckets.'

Nazeer pulls out a photo from the pile. It shows a young Munir, in sandals, shorts and a short coat, holding a bucket of water, a white Muslim cap on his head.

'There was no running water and, of course, there was no electricity or telephones. A man used to go around the main gates of the city at twilight with a ladder to add oil and light the lamps. We got electricity and telephone around 1930. I remember our first telephone number. It was 755. The old telegram addresses used to be Darul Aman and later Hindustan. And our post box number was 45. We still have it; in the main post office on Jaffa

Road. The manager of that post office was an Indian, a Bengali gentleman called Haldar.'

'Indian?'

'Yes, I remember at least three Indian families at that time when I was a young boy. They were all living outside the Old City. This man Haldar had a Christian wife from Jerusalem and a maidservant who was a Muslim. It was in his house that I first saw a toilet with a flush. I remember visiting that toilet and not knowing how to use the flush. I had to call in Mariam, who was there with me, and my father into the toilet to help me. We did not have such a toilet at home. My father's toilet looked like it belonged to the stone age.'

I wait for him to enjoy the moment, the humour of what must have been an intensely embarrassing situation for a young boy then. But I don't want to lose the trail of the other Indians, so I egg him on.

'And who were the other Indians?'

'The second was a Muslim man, a tailor, called Hajji Alamuddin from Punjab with a Palestinian wife. He was a famous tailor, making uniforms for the British army. He was so famous that he was called to the hotel of King Feisal, who was visiting Jerusalem, and asked to make the king's military suit. I went to his house too with my father. It was there that I saw my first refrigerator. And the third family was of Hajji Salim, who was actually Alamuddin's brother and a big contractor for the British army. I used to ask my father—Baba, why don't we get these things, a proper toilet, a car, a refrigerator—but he did not want to appear rich. He thought it would not look good to the people around him. He did not think that was the right way for a sheikh to live.'

'What happened to these families?'

'They left for Libya in 1948 when Israel was born. The areas which they lived in, near the present King David Hotel, and areas such as the German Colony were owned by rich Arab families. They all sold their properties to the Jews through agents in Cyprus; the Indians must have done the same.'

At night, in my room at the American Colony Hotel, I turn to an essay based on the diaries of Wasif Jawhariyyeh, born in an Eastern Orthodox family, who grew up to be one of Jerusalem's most illustrious citizens in the early twentieth century—composer, oud player, poet and chronicler. Wasif talks of a time when the city was growing beyond the old walls. The neighbourhoods of Sheikh Jarrah, Yemin Moshe and Wariyyeh had already been established; other neighbourhoods were coming up along the Jaffa Road. Hundreds of families began to move out of the old alleys into modern, tiled buildings.

It was the time too when the wonders of science began to emerge. Electricity was first introduced in the Notre Dame compound that lies just opposite the New Gate of the Old City. Wasif saw his first moving images in shocked wonderment at the Russian compound and his first automobile, a horseless car or quite simply a 'Ford' on Jaffa Road, driven by a certain Mr Vester, owner of the American Colony. That would have been the grandfather of Nick Vester, one of the owners of the hotel today, an intelligent, personable man who spends his time between Jerusalem and London, and one day turned up at my house with the whimsical Munther, introducing himself as he came.

Being an accomplished oud player himself, Wasif also writes knowingly of the emergence of popular Palestinian singers and performers hastened by the appearance in Jerusalem's cafés of the new music machines: the cylindrical wax machine followed by the hand-wound gramophone that played 78-rpm vinyl records. At the beginning of the First World War only a handful of such machines existed and cost about twenty-five French pounds each.

But during the war, the number expanded and café owners began to display this prized possession, often covered with red velvet to keep away the evil eye, using them as the latter-day jukebox, playing requests against the payment of a 'matleek', the smallest Ottoman coin.

These diaries unveil a new image of Jerusalem in the early twentieth century. Not as a joyless, puritanical city but one which also housed at least a section of the population given to hedonistic living with tales of drinking, smoking drugs, housing concubines in apartments of pleasure, all-night bachelor parties... Playing the oud at the gatherings of the socially elite members of Jerusalem's patrician families, usually at the special houses kept for their mistresses, Wasif had a unique vantage point for observing these activities and does not hesitate to recount them. He also lists several 'odahs' or bachelors' apartments not unlike the French garçonièrre. These were apartments kept by young men from the well-established families of the Old City for evenings spent playing cards, drinking, smoking arghilleh and bringing in prostitutes once in a while.

Wasif's family became more fully a part of this hedonistic nightlife when they opened the Café Jawhariyyeh in 1918 near the Russian compound. Here they gathered pleasure-seekers, cabaret dancers, singers around a menu of meze, arrack and iced water, the last being made possible by the coming of electricity.

Amid all this breathless excitement, Wasif does touch upon one Indian connection. He describes an incident when, in 1919, at the very beginning of the British Mandate, he, a Christian, passed himself off as a Muslim to the Indian guards of the Haram area while his companion, a blue-eyed Muslim, was barred because Wasif passed him off as a Jew!

I turned to sleep with visions of the young Munir wandering in the alleyways of the Old City, absorbed in amazed awe after his encounters with modern toilets and refrigerators while, unknown to him, a hedonistic Jerusalem had been living and breathing excitedly outside the old walls, even ten years before he was born.

12

Manager of the Chhota Club

What turned the Indian Hospice, a refuge for pilgrims, into a leave camp for war-weary soldiers? I turn to Ilan Pappé's *A History of Modern Palestine* to learn what was happening in the area when the Second World War broke out. 'The Second World War,' he writes, 'affected Palestine at various times and with differing intensity, with Rommel's speedy progress in North Africa generating a web of rumours of a possible Nazi occupation, of Italian air bombardment of the coastal towns, and of flirtation between the Axis powers and the Palestinian leadership... But more than anything else, the war was made visible by an unprecedented number of British soldiers and military personnel in the land, turning it into a vast logistics centre. It should be stressed that, unlike in the First World War, Palestine was not a war zone. Instead, it was an enormous army camp, which both increased the number of foreign soldiers and provided jobs.'

An enormous army camp—and a part of this camp, a leave camp for Indian soldiers fighting in the area, was the Indian Hospice in Jerusalem. I wonder who these soldiers were. In response, Sheikh Munir mentions one day that they were perhaps from the 4 Infantry division. A little research about the division reveals the following entry:

> The Indian 4 Infantry Division was raised as an infantry division of the British Indian Army. The division was formed in Egypt in 1939 and was the first Indian formation to go overseas during the Second World War. As with other formations in the Indian Army prior to independence, it primarily had British officers and Indians in other ranks. However, it did include Indian officers with ranks as high as Captain or Major. During WWII, it took part in campaigns in East Africa (Eritrea and Sudan), Syria, North Africa and Italy. During World War II the Division captured 150,000 prisoners and suffered 25,000 casualties, more than the strength of a whole division. It won over 1,000 Honours and Awards which included 4 Victoria Crosses and 3 George Crosses.

The division had for its badge the picture of a swooping red eagle on a black background and that lineage is kept alive today by a division called Red Eagle in the Central Command of the Indian army.

Another day and I sit and watch the sun play hide-and-seek on the terrace outside my room in the King David Hotel in Jerusalem. It's a well-known hotel, its walls are full of pictures of the great and famous, its lobby has tiles with the names of celebrities. But for me its main attraction is the reading room with its old black-and-white photographs, from a time when the hotel was new, an icon of West Jerusalem, standing tall amidst the empty spaces or rolling hills. And when, as headquarters of the British army, it was a target—the extremist Zionist gang, Irgun, blew up its southern wing in 1946 in retaliation for the British refusal to allow a hundred thousand survivors of Nazi concentration camps into Palestine. I sip my coffee and wait for Sheikh Ansari and his family to join me for evening tea and I watch the magical warm light that reflects off the old walls of the Old City, from Jaffa Gate, from the cloisters and seminaries of the Armenian quarter, from the Dormition Abbey with its grey dome. A cloud darkens the Mount of Olives beyond and the steeples become silhouettes even in the late afternoon. I chase away the huge grey-breasted, grey-necked crow that tries to bully the sparrows who visit my terrace, looking for crumbs left over from breakfast.

As they walk in and settle down in the terrace café, they are a picture of friendly elegance. The girls—Najam, Nourjahan and Wafa—are stylishly dressed for the occasion. They like to come to King David Hotel, they say. They come to have a good time; good times are so rare nowadays. Even before she settles down, Najam changes the mood.

'I wonder how people laugh so much,' she says.

'But you laugh all the time,' I say, only half in jest.

'I only laugh till my face, not on the inside,' she says.

The sheikh himself walks in slowly. He is wearing a cream windcheater and walks tall, ramrod straight and proud as usual but seems to be dragging his foot. He embraces me, first one side and then the other and then back to the first. Now we always greet each other that way, unforced, affectionately.

We talk of his grandchildren, one who may go to Hebrew University and the other who does not want to go away to the US. But eventually we begin to talk of the hotel and from that it is only a short step to the time when it was bombed, when it was the headquarters of the British army, when Indian soldiers used to come to rest and recuperate at the Indian Hospice.

'They were fighting in different places—Tripoli, Benghazi, Tobruk, El Alamein...' says Sheikh Munir, 'and they used to come to spend their leave in Jerusalem, in the Indian zawiya. There was a permanent staff of one hundred and fifty people stationed there, including a 'mochi' and a 'darzi'. There were two kitchens running, one for the Muslims and Christians and another for the Hindus and Sikhs. Three sheep were slaughtered daily for each kitchen. The three for the Muslims and Christians would be slaughtered in the hospice in the halal tradition and the three for the Sikhs and Hindus would be slaughtered as 'jhatka' but not in the hospice. My father did not allow that, so they used to be slaughtered in the Allenby barracks.

'I was about sixteen during the war years, just out of school and doing nothing. There was a Major Ajwani who asked me if I would like to work. I said all right. He then took me to NAAFI—the Naval, Army, Air Force Institute. I became a salesman at the shop they had there. I used to sell cigarettes, chocolates and so on. There were other branches too—at the Augusta Victoria and at Qalandiya. I worked in all three places over the next five years. Then they opened up a small place in the hospice itself. They called it the YMCA Chhota Club. They even put up a board saying that. I was made the manager of the Chhota Club! I did that for a year or so. My father was made an honorary captain but he did not wear the uniform. Mariam too got a rank of a welfare officer and she did wear the uniform!

'That was a wonderful time for us. I learnt Urdu from one of the soldiers and taught him Arabic in return. In fact my Urdu was so good then that I surprised my cousins when I went to meet them in 1950.'

He does not mention what I have seen in some of the old photographs. The times when he, a young teenager with wavy hair, borrowed and rode a motorcycle of one of the army officers. Later on I discover the motorcycle belonged to one Subedar Musharafullah.

'When the army left, they left us two wings that they built

in the hospice—the Travancore wing and the Delhi Manzil. The Travancore is where I stay, since 1967, and the Delhi wing is with the UNRWA.'

I have seen the UNRWA office and clinic there. The organization came to the hospice in 1948 and rented the building as a distribution centre of milk and food for the Palestinians who became refugees that year. Later, the place became a clinic. The people who still come there are the refugees of 1948. They carry with them their valuable refugee cards and hand them from generation to generation. In fact a few of such families had actually moved into the Indian Hospice for a few years. The clinic has been steadily improved. The Delhi Manzil, built in 1943, is now the clinic for children and the other side, which used to be a kitchen for the soldiers during the war years, has now been improved to house a dentist and a diabetician. Three to four hundred patients from the refugee families still come every day to the clinic but the staff nurse has told me that the numbers have dropped since the wall—or the separation barrier—came up around the West Bank and made access to Jerusalem that much more difficult. Beyond the clinic I can see an overgrown passage, crowded with old furniture, leading to a side entrance of the hospice. It is through this passage that Jewish settlers once came in, in a vain attempt to occupy the Indian Hospice.

After they leave, I sit for a while on the terrace outside my room trying to imagine what the life of the manager of the Chhota Club must have been like in the war years. The sun has set and very soon things will become dark. There is no light reflecting off the old walls of the city, just the walls as they are, pale stone cooling off after a day of fierce sunlight. The mounts of Scopus and Olives are already being swallowed up by the twilight and I have a feeling that church bells will start ringing soon. Below me, French tourists are eating on the terrace; a foursome struggles on the tennis court; and beyond, on a patch of green next to the pines, a young juggler practises with three batons as his girlfriend takes pictures. The flags flutter briskly in the evening breeze—the European flag, the French flag, many Israeli flags, and in the Old City, white and yellow flags atop various Christian seats of power.

Sheikh Nazir Ansari, in a letter written in 1949, has left a detailed account of how the hospice served as a leave camp for the Indian soldiers. Except for removing obvious typos I have quoted extensively from this letter below so that none of its underlying emotion and proximity to events is lost in any way. Sheikh Nazir insists that there was a single kitchen for the troops though the reality may have been slightly different at least as far as the cooking of meat was concerned, to which Munir's memory about jhatka and halal testifies.

> ...When the 2nd world war broke out, the pilgrims stopped coming from India and the funds went short and I had to pass very bad times owing to financial difficulty and the Ottoman Fund of Pounds 10/- being insufficient to carry on such big institution, I and my wife offered our services to the Military Headquarters to make leave camps for the Middle East Indian army, who used to stay in the Indian Hospice and served the Indian Army as Welfare Officers. When the military authorities saw our work and they were so much pleased that they constructed many building in the India Hospice along with the big water tanks and all facilities with the clear understanding that after the war is over the building structures will remain in tact and will be handed over to the Indian Hospice. In war time every time about 500 Military Officers and other ranks used to stay in this institution to pass their vacation in Jerusalem. We served the Indian units day and night till 1947 when

the troops left Palestine for India. This period was about eight years from 1940 to 1947. During that period many Generals, Princes, Maharajas & Nawabs visited this welfare centre and were very much pleased to see this centre and left credentials which I can produce on demand. Special beauty was that in this centre there was no caste and religion question and all the troops to eat from the same kitchen and all the types were treated here equally without distinction. I and my wife used to hold lectures among the troops how to remain united and instruct then that India is more dearer to every Indian than their religion. The result was that all the troops used to share their meals from the same kitchen. I and my wife used to visit weekly Indian units in Palestine to lecture them and teach them how to remain united as real Indians and tell that the nation is first and then religion. The highest military authorities appreciated my and my wife's work and left every time very good notes in the official visitors book of the Indian Hospice. In this way the Indian Hospice was run. When Shrimati Kamla Devi Chattopadia visited Indian Hospice, she was very much pleased and she said that this Indian corner must be maintained at any cost. In 1947 when the Indian troops left and war was over, the local troubles started, the result was when the British withdrew from Palestine, the Arabs and Jews declared war. In 1948 in the month of May the regular war was started, the result was that all Arabs left Palestine. I and my wife along with my children stayed in the Indian Hospice because we thought that by leaving the institution the whole institution will be ruined and no door or window would have been left. We put our life into the danger where whole night bombs and shells were in the Indian Hospice. In one night 1700

> shells and bombs were thrown in the Indian hospice from the Jew side, as the institution was in the centre of the old city. The result was that many buildings were damaged and cracked and mostly all the glasses of the building broken.
>
> After working day and night to make such a beautiful Indian corner, I did not care for my life or my family and children life for sake of such wonderful institution worth at least Sterling two hundred thousand to be ruined. It means my labour of 25 years would have been lost forever. In August 1948, the International Red Cross started to feed the Arab refugees. They tried their best to find out a building for them in Jerusalem. No Arab came forward to give them any portion of the buildings. I wanted to keep the name of India and came forward to offer them the some part of institution to serve and feed Arab refugees of Jerusalem. Till today our hospice is one of the biggest centres from where the food and other essentials articles are being distributed to Arab refugees of Jerusalem. [...] In this Indian Hospice there is no distinction of any caste and religion and every Indian has a right to take advantage of such an institution. I being an Indian it is a duty of mine to keep the Indian nation name up and maintain this institution at any cost. In Jerusalem there are many Hospices such as French, Italian, German, Russian, British, Ethiopian and many other nations. So it is in the interest of India to maintain such a place. The Indian Hospice is like a model town.

From the several testimonials left in the records of the hospice of the work done by Sheikh Nazir and his wife Mariam, I will pick the one written by Maj. S.A. Hashumi, private secretary to H.H. Nawab, ruler of Bahawalpur State on 27 December 1942.

> It gives me great pleasure to put on record my sincere gratitude to Sheikh Nazir Hasan Ansari and Mrs Ansari. They both have really been doing a great service to their countrymen, a service to those who come to this holy land for pilgrimage and a service to those brave sons of India who have [come] out of their country to fight for a great cause, for the King and for the Great Empire, of which Indians are also a component part.
>
> At Mr Ansari's invitation I shifted to the Indian Zawia from the King David Hotel just for a night to see things with my own eyes and it gave immense pleasure to express how much I was impressed to see the Ansari couple working for the comfort of Indian N.C.O.s and rank about fifty of whom had turned up to the zawiya that night. They were from Bhopal, Rampur and Indian troops and Mrs Ansari the kind hostess was busy in managing for their comforts till 12'o'clock. It was Xmas night, she worked hard till midnight and next morning I came to know that she gave birth to a child. This gives one an idea of the most motherly way in which the lady looks after the soldiers of her country, even in such a delicate time. The husband I found a scholar and really good organizer. I think he deserves a great encouragement in the work he has undertaken for the comforts of the Indian soldiers…

What it would mean to a battle-weary soldier to come across a place like the Indian Hospice when least expected is summed up in another visitor's entry, one Captain D.A. Sirdhyan.

> …After a long spell of absence from India and passing through various theaters of war, an opportunity is given to me for a short leave to visit Palestine. There is a great feeling of relief at the knowledge of Indian Hospice, where

> one gets peace of mind at the sight of Shaikh addressing you in Hindustani and the charm of which suddenly falls upon ears who had experienced foreign accent for a quite long time.
>
> He has proved himself to be an able guide and sound knowledge of historic events and none can explain better to an Indian than him. The luxury of having an Indian meal can best be enjoyed here...

It was quite clear that while Sheikh Nazir and his wife toiled to make the soldiers at home, they were not anywhere close to converting the hospice to an army barrack: Sheikh Nazir had obviously made it clear that the original character of the hospice would not change. Only this assumption explains the detailed letter written by Maj. G. Stephenson, director of the Army Welfare Services in June 1946 to Sheikh Nazir putting on record the principles on the basis of which the hospice was being used, lest there be any confusion in the mind of his successors. I quote below an extensive excerpt:

> 3. First it is fully realized that the Indian hospice is trust property controlled by the Waqf department and that leave parties are regarded by you as 'pilgrims in service dress'.
> 4. A certain number of Indian soldiers must reside there in order to act as cooks, clerks and to supervise general administration.
> 5. It is, however, emphasized that:
>
>   a) no building or structural alteration to accommodate leave personnel may be made without your authority.
>   b) that no alcoholic drink shall be consumed in the premises.

> c) that civilians wishing to use the hospice mosque for prayer will do so freely.
>
> d) that goat or sheep will only be killed in a halel [sic] method and the Jatka method.
>
> e) that in the event of Moslem pilgrims coming from India or elsewhere, accommodation will be made available at the hospice and the pilgrims entertained by you.
>
> f) that all Army personnel residing at the hospice shall protect the right and property of the hospice and that any instance of bad behaviour should be reported immediately to the officer in charge.
>
> This HQ is very appreciative of the facilities so generously offered by the Hospice and has no desire to offend any civilian worshipper.

And in May 1947, when the troops were finally ready to leave, the two dormitories built by them—the Travancore and Delhi wings—were handed over to Sheikh Nazir Ansari. The letter from the adjutant general's branch of the Army HQ in New Delhi, recording this handover, also mentions that the Government of India should be informed that 'should there ever be occasion for Indian troops to be stationed in Palestine again, then two excellent leave dormitories are already erected in Jerusalem for their use.'

It was in 1947 too that Sheikh Munir managed to convince his father to allow him to bring his mother and sisters back into the hospice.

'I told my father, yaani, it is now time. My sisters are grown up and they need to be here. He resisted—it was because of my stepmother of course—but finally he agreed to give us one room. And I had to pay him rent! Not only that I had to sign an agreement with him that there would be no trouble between us and my stepmother or her children. Only then were we allowed to come back.'

There is anger and there is hurt in his voice, and I look away as he goes silent.

13

The Turkish Seeker of the Abode of the Indians

It's Friday afternoon and West Jerusalem is preparing to close for Sabbath. An Orthodox Jewish tailor fumbles with the lock on the door of his shop at the corner of King George Street as I hurry to find the bookshop where a volume of Evliya Çelebi's travelogue, his *Seyahatname*, is waiting for me, reserved over the phone.

But I need not have worried. The shop is in a street where the Friday flea market is still thriving. I resist the temptations of bottles of kibbutz wine, glass beads and necklaces, artefacts made of polished olive wood and find the bookshop. After picking up the slim volume, I am reluctant to leave and scour the shelves for an hour or more for travelogues, maps, pilgrim accounts...anything that could give one more hint, open up another path towards the connection of India or Indians with this city.

But nothing more presents itself and, loaded with two novels which I have really no need for and in all probability will never end up reading, I move towards the Old City whose stone walls, steeples and domes are resplendent in the hot afternoon sun. The jacaranda is in heartbreaking bloom. But my thoughts are with Çelebi and his travels in Jerusalem; it's the same place, but another time.

Born in 1611 in Constantinople, Evliya Çelebi (or Evliya

Mehmed Zilli bin Dervish) travelled for over thirty years through seventeen countries. He made two trips to Palestine—first towards the end of 1649 and again in 1670–71 when he continued to Mecca to perform hajj. The ten-volume *Seyahatname* contains descriptions of these journeys in inexhaustible detail. The slim volume that I have picked up, with its grainy cream cover, a lithograph of pilgrims riding near the Dead Sea on its front cover and another of a Turkish horseman on its back, is only a part of this massive work. Entitled *Travels in Palestine (1648-1650)*, it obviously refers only to his first journey. But it's enough for me; it contains an ineluctable lodestone: a seventeenth-century mention of Indians in the Old City, of the Zawiya al-Hindiya. I have been hooked by the sentences that I found on leafing quickly through it: 'The portico at the Gate of Mary, which looks north, is the abode of Indians.' A couple of paragraphs later, he writes: 'The total number of madrassas in Jerusalem amounts to some three hundred and sixty madrassas and zawiya, both large and small. Yet the madrassa which is the best and the most cared for is that of Bab Hutta.'

Çelebi records, in the second century of Ottoman rule, that the pasha of Jerusalem had five hundred soldiers at his command and was the commandant of the pilgrims' caravan of Damascus. He was the leader of the Mecca pilgrims to (or does he mean *from?*) Damascus and back, receiving for his efforts an annuity of forty thousand piastres. Jerusalem was a prosperous province yet its fief-holders did not serve in the field but only accompanied and conducted the pilgrims to the place of pilgrimage. He goes on to describe the legal and bureaucratic set-up. As an interesting footnote, he adds that there are 'seven resplendent *awqaf* in Jerusalem, the *mutevelliler* (trustees) of which attend the court, each coming there with a present for the Molla.' He does not list which these seven are but given the number of references to Indian dervishes in his text, it would be safe to presume that the Indian Hospice must surely have been one of them.

Çelebi has, I soon decipher, a fondness for round figures. Jerusalem, he writes, was besieged a hundred times before the huge walls were built by the Turkish Sultans. Clutching his slim volume that Sabbath afternoon I climb the ramparts of these walls near Jaffa Gate. Çelebi calls this gate Bab Khalil al-Rahman, or the Gate of the Friend of the Compassionate i.e. Abraham. It is the gate through which General Allenby entered in 1917 accompanied by Indian soldiers. And this too was the gate that was barred from 1948 to 1967 and beyond which, during those years, lay the swampy no man's land between Israel and Jordan. Today that area is the most expensive in West Jerusalem.

An ample passage allows one to walk comfortably on top of the wide wall built of huge ashlars or dressed stones, 'each ashlar having the size of a lion or the hind-parts of an elephant.' As he proceeded to what was known to him as the Gate of the Iron Warmace or alternatively, the Bozdoghan Qapu, named so ever since a Kurdish wrestler was executed there, Çelebi had a view of gardens and orchards. This is the Damascus Gate of today, also called in Arabic as the Bab al-Nasr, the Gate of Victory, alluding to the triumphal entry of Saladin into the city. This multiplicity of names for the different gates of the city and also the gates or porticoes that lead on to the Haram al-Sharif or Temple Mount is a source of much confusion to anyone trying to follow old accounts.

But whatever the name of the gate, from where I stand there are no gardens or orchards to be seen on either side. Towards the west I see the buildings of modern West Jerusalem, the seat of the Israeli government with its courts and Knesset, hotels and apartment blocks, all of the uniform sand-coloured Jerusalem stone. Towards the north are the more crowded, less developed neighbourhoods of East Jerusalem. And to my right, inside the Old City are the backyards of restaurants and hotels, the courtyards of the patriarchate and monasteries of the Christian quarter. The view from atop Damascus Gate also tells me that somewhere I have crossed the invisible but unmistakable line between West and East Jerusalem: while the West is descending quickly into the solemn silence of Sabbath, the East is alive with the almost constant stream of people leaving Damascus Gate after the Friday prayers at the Al-Aqsa Mosque. The traffic slows down to a crawl to allow this stream to pass. Women in black robes, heads covered, old men with wizened faces and grizzly beards laughing, chattering, hurrying into the crowded lanes, past the kabab shops with skewered chicken hearts and livers roasting slowly on red-hot coals.

Another four hundred paces, according to Çelebi, and I am standing atop the Bab al-Zahira or Herod's Gate. If I look inwards into the Old City, I am looking right into the compound of the Indian Hospice, the nearest buildings being those which house the UNRWA clinic. At the extreme corner, a relatively unkempt and overgrown corner, is a rough structure and my first guess is that it is some sort of a tomb. I make a mental note to ask Sheikh Munir about it some day.

As I wind myself down the iron staircase to the arch of Herod's Gate where the vegetable- and fruit-sellers have gathered in full strength, Nazeer is waiting for me outside the familiar green gate with its crescent moon. Known as Sadeq Gate, it was put up in 1942 and was in danger of being pushed back once when the authorities wanted, in the immediate aftermath of the 1967 takeover, to put in a little circle just inside Herod's Gate. Mercifully the plan was given up.

'The portico at the Gate of Mary, which looks north, is the abode of Indians... The total number of madrassas in Jerusalem amounts to some three hundred and sixty madrassas and zawiya, both large and small. Yet the madrassa which is the best and the most cared for is that of Bab Hutta.'

Those throwaway lines of Çelebi, written nearly four hundred years ago, raise many questions, questions which I drill again and again into Nazeer as he smiles gently and starts walking me away from the gate of the hospice. Where exactly is this Gate of Mary? What abode did Çelebi mean? And did he refer to Bab Hutta as merely one of the gates to the Haram al-Sharif or to the entire area beyond the northern wall of the Haram, since both the gate and the area carry the same name? And was he referring to the Indian Hospice that I know as the best of its time?

We turn right along the periphery of the hospice, past the shops that were built in the early sixties with the help of the Indian government to provide rent and funds to the hospice. Only one level could be built before the war of 1967 intervened and put paid to the idea of building a guest house on the second level. There is a butcher, a grocer, a photographer... From across the road a group of men watch with an indefinable mix of curiosity and idleness. They are sitting in a ramshackle café, rolling dice, prayer beads in one hand, the other stretching towards their narghile pipes, small glasses of coffee on low tables in front of them. Nazeer senses the temptation gurgling in my steps.

'You don't want to go there,' he warns. 'Everything that is shady happens there...'

He persuades me to hurry past the café and points to the first two shops. 'This was where my father opened a company with his brothers: Ansari Trading Co. It was a side business for a few years, from 1964 to 1967. He went to Moradabad and got an agency for brassware. They also got agencies for tea and spices. These two shops had a board 'Nimala' after my youngest sister and they were decorated in Indian style with pictures of the Taj, even selling saris. It was good business, he was a supplier for many other shops in

Jerusalem. But it all ended with 1967.'

In a few minutes he announces, 'We are already in Bab Hutta. This entire area is called by that name. Let me show you another property that is also with the Indian Hospice.'

I have never heard of this before. With mounting excitement I follow him through the narrow lanes. Young Arab boys are tossing a black and white football around, others shoot at each other with water guns. There are grapes on iron trellises on ancient walls, there are watchful cats on impossible perches. It is evident that in these lanes outsiders are viewed with suspicion. Yet, occasionally, I hear a snatch of a Hindi song thrown in my direction as an acknowledgement of recognition, friendship, acceptance.

A boy, barely five or so, drags half a cycle through the narrow lane—it has no rear wheel. As I glance up at the narrow corridor of pale blue sky that is the roof of this lane, I see an inexplicable sight that I am to see often in the Muslim quarter of the Old City: a pair of canvas shoes hangs from the electricity wires that criss-cross the patch of sky in the lane, evidence both of the lack of municipal attention to proper wiring and, at the same time, of the randomness of the existence of the youth who can pass an idle hour throwing his canvas shoes just right.

We come suddenly to the property that Nazeer referred to, at the dead end of an uphill stretch. It is a large house and obviously several families are staying in it. The entrance is an arched lobby lined with old stones, out of which low entrances open into the inner courtyard.

'It has been with the hospice a long time. Rich merchants who came as pilgrims to the city must have bought it and added it to the endowment of the hospice,' Nazeer explains as he surveys the inner courtyard, a worried expression clouding his face. The wall has been freshly cemented, rooms have recently been added on. A net of criss-crossing wires and mushrooming satellite dishes add to the feeling of being hemmed in.

We move towards the second property; we are still in Bab Hutta and we are constantly moving closer to the Haram al-Sharif, closer to the Gate of Mary. Çelebi seems to be smiling under his beard at us from across the centuries. It is a most unusual property. All one can see at first glance is a corner shop and a huge raised backyard, fenced off with a high wall and a bamboo curtain. From the second-floor window of the house across the narrow lane, a man hails Nazeer. He is a cousin and soon he is with us; his family watches from the window. We climb a ladder attached to the wall and then clamber over. An amazing sight awaits us. In the middle of the crowded Old City is an open stretch of two 'dunams', or two thousand square metres. And it houses a mini-zoo, surrealistically set amidst the surrounding landscape of black water tanks and satellite dishes. There are at least four different coloured peacocks, including several white ones, turkeys, ducks, hens, black swans.

'We are lucky that we have our cousin constantly watching over the property for the hospice,' Nazeer says. 'Otherwise an open stretch like this in the old city is begging to be encroached. We got a letter from the muncipality, asking us if we would agree to make this a public garden without changing the ownership. We declined, but maybe in the long run we have to start something here. We once made plans for a kindergarten but did not have the money.'

Resisting insistent invitations to join the family for coffee, we move towards the third property. We are still in the Bab Hutta area. Nazeer suddenly stops before a low door and tries its handle. It is locked.

'This is a bakery; it is also part of the endowment of the hospice,' says Nazeer, smiling at my surprised expression.

Hugging the eastern wall of the city is a narrow and long

plot of land with a low house in it. A gate opens when Nazeer knocks but the man he asks for is not at home. A green garden with grapevines climbing the stone walls provides a hint of the promise that is inside.

'This house is now occupied by the head of the gypsy community of Jerusalem. They are good tenants for the hospice; they always pay their rent.'

I wonder how long these properties have been with the Indian Hospice and for how long Indian pilgrims have been coming here. Perhaps they were here even when Çelebi was travelling around, crowding this quarter of Bab Hutta, while Sufi dervishes performed their prayers and zikr in view of the Dome of the Rock.

As we walk along to the end of the plot of land, we are almost at the northern porticoes of the Haram and on our left stands one of the Old City's gates of which Çelebi says: 'The building near this gate is believed to be the birthplace of Mary. Hence this gate is also called the Gate of Mary.' It's a huge gate that leads out of the city towards the east; it has many other names: the Gate of the Tribes, St Stephen's Gate and, most popularly today, Lions' Gate after the lions carved in the stone above the arch. It is the gate that faces the Mount of Olives, the gate through which I have seen the Christians march at Easter, coming down from the Mount, past the Garden of Gethsemane and through the Via Dolorosa, carrying crosses, singing hymns, remembering the Passion of Christ. It is also the gate in front of which some Indian soldiers posed for a photograph during the First World War. That photo can be found in many souvenir shops in the Old City.

I cannot enter the Haram al-Sharif from the portico near Lions' Gate; it is only open to the Muslims who are going in for the evening prayer. The Israeli guards check their identity cards and their bags and shrug nonchalantly when I ask permission to take a photograph.

I persist with Çelebi a while longer and walk along the Via Dolorosa, past the first and second stations of the Cross. On the lane that leads on to the Bab Hutta portico is an arch that stretches across the Via Dolorosa. Small rooms with barred windows have been made on top of the arch.

'My father wanted you to see this arch,' says Nazeer. 'When he was not living in the hospice but outside with his mother, grandmother and younger sisters, they stayed for five years in these rooms.' The barred windows begin to speak. They tell of desperation, deprivation, estrangement.

Past this arch is the third portico to the Haram which Çelebi calls the Bab al-Nazir. Today the gate is called after King Feisal. It lies, according to Çelebi, 'just behind the Palace of the Pasha.'

I look closely at the building that could have been this palace. A high arched doorway marks it with distinction. I recognize it as one of the doorways pictured in a poster titled 'The Doorways of Jerusalem' that I have seen in Munther's bookshop.

The heavy door is slightly ajar and I peep in. A large courtyard surrounded by rooms, staircases going to the roof... A man steps out and walks past me, indifferent. I ask him whether he knows what this building was in the past. He shrugs and walks away into the twilight; history sometimes leaves no traces.

Back on the Via Dolorosa, the door of the Al Omariya School is open and we step in gingerly. Two paintings of Caliph Omar on the facing wall greet us. I recognize the courtyard from the photographs I have seen in the hospice. Here is where the Islamic Conference took place in the thirties, and here Sheikh Nazir Ansari stood in a group that included the mufti of Palestine and the Khilafat leader, Shauqat Ali. In the falling dusk we step up to the windows that look on to the Haram. The golden Dome seems near enough to reach out and touch and the last rays of the sun have given it a warm glow. The call for the Maghrib prayer of dusk adds a magic touch. In the other direction, across the Via Dolorosa, two Christian crosses atop two domes are silhouetted against a darkening sky still splattered with pink.

I am yearning to sit down somewhere and have a coffee and jot down my notes. But Nazeer has other plans. This is the street of the hospices, it seems. We are right there by the Uzbek Hospice. It used to be a full running hospice right up until 1967 with the prominent citizen Sheikh Bukhari at its head. It belonged to one of the most important of Sufi orders—the Naqshbandis, an order which preferred the silent remembrance of God to the musical devotion of other orders.

'Unfortunately,' says Nazeer, 'he died a few years ago. He was buried inside the hospice. It used to be the tradition.'

He doesn't hesitate to step into the open door; I notice he is so familiar with the city that he does not hesitate to step in anywhere. A narrow metal staircase winds upwards to the first floor and on the ground floor is a small mosque. We step out again.

'This mosque was not there earlier,' Nazeer tells me. 'The property fell on bad times. There were problems within the family and this part which was a shop has now been converted into a mosque. This happens many times in this area now. If people don't want a property to be confiscated or encroached upon, they convert it into a mosque.

'The rest of the property has gone back to the awqaf department, something that happens when there is nobody left to look after a zawiya's property.'

The Uzbek Hospice stretches almost up to another portico to the Haram. It's the last of the porticoes on the north wall—the Bab al-Ghawanmeh. It is a small gate, only the inhabitants of the surrounding houses use it for going and coming from the mosque. Two Israeli guards sit in its alcove against the unlikely backdrop of an old blocked doorway, its shoulders decorated with blue ceramic tiles with designs of birds and vines and flowers. Above the doorway is a plaque from somewhere in the past that reads: 'Rest House of the Dome of the Rock'. But from the look of the doorway, that rest house has been locked for a very long time.

From that small gate we turn right up a narrow staircase into a narrow lane. The second house belongs to Nazeer's maternal grandparents. It is the house where his mother was born, where he used to play around as a child. It was from this house that the young Sheikh Munir took away his bride Ikram in 1953, his companion of nearly six decades who now sits quietly listening whenever we gather to hear his stories. There is a quiet understanding between them and a silent communication. She allows him to speak, smiling or nodding occasionally, rarely speaking. But it's obvious that she follows every word that is being said, remembers every story that is being retold, sometimes better than him.

'And this,' Nazeer is pointing out, 'is the Afghan Hospice.' Over a firmly closed green door I see a plaque that announces 'Al Zawiyah Afghania 1043 hijri'. The hospice looks very closed and he pushes the green door but this one does not give way. Its stone walls curve around far into a lane. Inside there are houses and a very nice garden, he tells me. There is a group which inhabits the hospice and he has heard them dance and pray. But the place no longer functions as a hospice.

Another gentle curve in the lane and we are behind the Armenian Hospice. It is a new building and the place looks very much in business, very well looked after. It is just behind the church that marks the third and fourth stations on the Via Dolorosa. The Armenian Christians have a long and old presence in the city, going back to the first century after Christ, and an entire quarter of the city is named after them. It contains the Cathedral of St James, a patriarchate and a seminary for their bearded priests, and shops which sell pottery and tiles. And I recall an exciting cavernous restaurant below street level with ancient armour, samovars and chandeliers.

Across the street is the Austrian Hospice, by far the most imposing structure of all. It commands the corner intersection of the Via Dolorosa with the Al-Wad Street, the intersection that controls the two approaches from Damascus Gate and Lions' Gate and where a large number of Israeli border guards always seem to be lounging around, their guns seeming almost too heavy for them. Almost at their feet sit Arab women selling vegetables from small round baskets; a Palestinian boy smokes indolently behind his cartload of ka'ek.

We step up to the door past the Arab boys lounging nonchalantly on the steps and press the bell. The door opens, we go through a double door and up the steps into a leafy garden. Inside is a hotel, with lovely old chequerboard floors, paintings, photographs. A café has a self-service area in the garden and we can sit there if we can find space. It's known for its Sachertorte with whipped cream and apple strudel doused with powdered sugar. We sit under the trees, around an Armenian tiled table, savouring the delicacies. There is a brisk breeze and there are church bells all around.

'This was a hospital during 1967,' explains Nazeer. 'All of us were here for weeks recovering from our injuries.'

To me the hospice seems to have been here a long time and I wonder when it became a hospital and how long it stayed. A pamphlet kept at the reception, which I pick up as we leave, provides the answers. Established in 1857, the hospice served as the centre of Austria's cultural and political presence in Jerusalem till the First World War. Pilgrims began to return to it after the war years and a third floor had to be added in the thirties. During the Second World War, the property was confiscated by the British as German property and converted into an internment centre for German, Austrian and Italian priests, nuns and monks. With the departure of the British in 1948, the Jordanian authorities turned the place into first a military and then a civil hospital. This was finally closed down in 1985 when the Austrians again renovated the building to return it to its present form and function.

An unrelated recollection comes swiftly to my mind as I hurry through the darkening Via Dolorosa, emptying of pilgrims and tourists.

It's a dark tale told by Sari Nusseibeh in his book and then personally around a dinner table late one Tel Aviv night. It was on the Via Dolorosa that a young Sari, freshly returned from his studies abroad, set up home with his wife and young sons in a house once inhabited by a Sufi saint from Bukhara. I can see now that it must have been around the Uzbek Hospice. From this house, next to one of the porticoes to the Haram, he could look over to the Hill of Gethsemane or the Hill of Evil Counsel or turn to take in the magnificent view of the Dome of the Rock just behind the house. The Nusseibehs set up the Lemon Tree Café where young Palestinian and Israeli intelligentsia and backpackers could mingle in the shadow of stone walls redolent with history.

One cold night, Sari saw a young well-built German and his girlfriend leave the café and walk, cuddling together down the cobbled lane. A few minutes later, now up in his living room, he heard a muffled sound and a thud break the wintry silence of the night and then the sound of light steps walking away. It was the same German backpacker, shot in the neck with a silenced weapon. With the help of an Arab policeman, Sari half dragged, half carried the man to the hospital at the Austrian Hospice at the corner of the Via Dolorosa. The emergency room was on the third floor and there was no elevator. By the time they reached there, it was too late. The murder was never really solved, only ascribed vaguely to 'Arab terrorists'. Nor was the mystery of the girlfriend and the light steps that Sari heard quickly vanishing up the alley.

I too turn into that alley with Nazeer and climb the broad steps that will lead us back in a broad sweep to Herod's Gate and the Indian Hospice.

On the walk back, we marvel at Çelebi and his descriptions. Little seems to have changed in three hundred and fifty years. A name here or there, more people, a few cars, an empire or two gone back to dust—but other than that, he is spot on. To the north of the Haram was the abode of the Indians he said, and there it was. Probably in the madrasa over the northern porticoes and beyond, the pilgrims from India lived and prayed and fasted in the various properties belonging to the Zawiya al-Hindiya, spread over the narrow lanes of the Bab Hutta quarter of the city. And something must have made him conclude that this was the madrasa that was the best looked after amongst all of those present in seventeenth-century Jerusalem.

Suddenly my story of the Zawiya al-Hindiya has travelled back successfully three hundred and fifty years, and that much closer to Baba Sheikh Farid.

Over the months that follow, one by one, like doves carrying little messages, the documents float down from the records of the Jerusalem sharia court of the Ottoman times. These records, among the oldest files in the Middle East, were kept at the Tankaziya School, the headquarters of the court during Ottoman rule. In 1941 they were shifted to the Naqshbandia school and later to Salahdin Street. Finally they were moved into metal trunks and placed in a dome in the Al-Aqsa Mosque and later copied and maintained in almirahs in the Islamic university in Abu Dis. One by one they come, when least expected, in odd ways.

And one day there is a whole dovecote we discover, in the shape of excerpts from a book by Dr Ibrahim Rabaya'a which relies heavily on the sharia records as it traces the city's history in the seventeenth century. There is no need for conjecture any more. It is all written down there in black and white: Indians came to Jerusalem at various times, mostly for religious purposes or pilgrimage. Some stayed on in the city. The majority resided in Bab Hutta, and they had their own private courtyard known as the Indian courtyard. The records points out presence of Indians from various parts of India, e.g. Kashmir, Multan, Sindh... They all had sheikhs to represent them in matters dealing with authority. At times all the Indian groups were represented by one sheikh.

The Indians also had zawiyat in Jerusalem identified by their names; in that era more than one zawiya was known to belong to Indians in a number of Jerusalem neighbourhoods: Al-Niyaba, Al-Ghawanmeh, Bab al-Zahira and Beni Zaid. By way of further confirmation that there was more than one zawiya, the record shows that the sheikh of the zawiya in Bab al-Zahira (the one near Herod's Gate) in AD 1635 was Ismail Ibn Abid al-Nabi, while the Salmani zawiya sheikh that same year was Ishaq Ibn Sa'ad al-Din. Each of the zawiyat had a similar structure: residential rooms, a masjid, a room to wash hands and feet before prayers, a well and a cemetery where the sheikh of the zawiya and some of his followers lay buried.

More details are also available: the Salmani Indian waqf located by the courthouse near Bab al-Ghawanmeh, was completely damaged in AD 1687 and nothing was left except the mosque. While at the hospice near Bab al-Zahira—known as Zawiyat Sheikh Farid, headed then by the Indian Sheikh Ismail Ibn Abid al-Nabi, as well as Sheikh Ali Ibn Da'ud al-Malti—the mosque was renovated in AH 1098/AD 1687. There are details of properties kept for rent and those for housing pilgrims, and records of property swaps between the various zawiyat.

The walk has been worth it. I don't have to doubt any more

that in the 1600s Indians had a strong presence in Jerusalem, not only in one hospice that we know today but in several. Most of them were in the Bab Hutta area on the northern side of the Haram al-Sharif.

Evliya Çelebi, relentless traveller and meticulous observer, was dead right.

14

'As If It Were One of Eight Paradises'

One can probably find more accurate descriptions of the Haram al-Sharif of Jerusalem, as well as of the raised platform within it on which stands the Dome of the Rock, but for the sheer mood it creates, it's difficult to beat the one by Çelebi.

> The platform of the Holy Rock is a field covered with white marble, to begin with. From seven places doors lead to it. They are double-arched and have no door-leaves. On the east is a door with a single arch. By a flight of eighteen stone steps one ascends to the platform of the Holy Rock.
>
> The approach from the north is through three doorways, by stone staircases of twenty steps each. On the south there are three other arched doorways. They too have no door-leaves. Also through them access is gained by a flight of twenty steps each, leading up to the platform of the Holy Rock. Thus it may be reached from all sides. It is seven Mecca ells higher than the ground around it. For the sanctuary is situated like a palace amidst a verdant valley, with the Rock of Allah at its centre. The ground underneath is honeycombed with caves from one end to the other. It was in those caves that Solomon imprisoned the evil spirits. The traces of their fetters and chains are

> still visible. People who are courageous enough enter these caves and have a look round. It is a dark and frightful place. Even at present it is the sleeping-place of evil genii, and is completely filled with dust. Through splits in the doors one may peep into them. These caves are filled to the brim with skeletons. The Rock of Allah is above them. Its dome is called the white villa because it is covered with natural white marble. Persons weary and distressed will leave the sanctuary full of hope and joy (by God's permission). The Haram does away with grief.
>
> I have also measured the whole circumference of its raised platform. Its width is two hundred paces from east to west, another two hundred paces from the western side, while the southern and northern sides are each three hundred paces long. Thus reckoning the area of the platform of the Rock of Allah, the circumference of the precincts is one thousand paces. And in the centre of these thousand square paces the luminous dome rises into the sky.
>
> And that is all.

At last I enter the Noble Sanctuary or the Haram al-Sharif to see at first hand the Al-Aqsa Mosque and the golden Dome of the Rock, the Dome that has defined Jerusalem for me from the time I saw my first picture postcard of the city.

I enter from the northeastern portico, the nearest to what Çelebi called the Gate of Mary, the nearest to the Bab Hutta quarter, the nearest to the abode of Indians through the centuries, walking through the little bazaar that has been set up outside, selling vegetables, dry fruits, clothes and shoes. Nazeer has arranged a special permit which allows a non-Muslim to use this gate. The instructions, I will learn later, have come from a kind and academically minded director who sits in a small office, reached only by a labyrinthine staircase, just beyond the western walls of the Haram.

The Israeli-Arab guards wave us in and suddenly I am walking towards the mosque, in constantly changing light, among the olive and cypress trees that dot the entire esplanade. Haram al-Sharif, Temple Mount, Mount Moriah—by whatever name it may be called, this must surely be one of the most controversial and bitterly fought-over patches of land in the world. And also the most revered. For the Jews it is the site of their First and Second Temples, both long destroyed. For the Muslims, this is the third most holy place in the world, after Mecca and Medina, the site of the Prophet's night journey to the heavens. This, too, is the place that was personally cleansed by Caliph Omar when he uncovered the Rock after conquering Jerusalem for Islam, and five centuries later washed with rose water by Saladin to rid it of the sacrilege wreaked by the Crusaders.

I am all too aware that every step I take is on ground steeped in culture, tradition, religion, conflict.

When I was told that there would be a guide I imagined a soft-spoken, suitably reverential cleric, steeped in historical and theological detail. But the man who turns up could have starred in a spaghetti western. He is a large mustachioed man in a denim waistcoat with a matching cavalier manner. He does nothing to help me calm my nerves. He is in a hurry and clearly is not appreciative of my desire to stop often to take photographs as we walk.

'Later, later, photographs later,' is all that he will say and walk on ahead.

Despite his haste, I stop to snatch one quick one of the Golden Gate amidst the pines. Far beyond, across the valley, on the slopes of Mount of Olives I catch the glint of the bright sun on the golden onion domes of the Russian Orthodox church of Mary

Magdalene. The Golden Gate, or the Gate of Mercy, on our left has been sealed ever since anyone can remember and different dates are given since when. But certainly it has been closed for several centuries. It is this gate through which the Jews believe the Messiah, when he comes, will enter the Temple Mount, after those good souls buried on the Mount of Olives have been raised from their graves. And for the Muslims too this is the gate associated with the Last Judgement, so it is a privilege to be buried in the cemetery just beyond it.

In Çelebi's days the dervishes of the order of Yazid al-Bistami lived in a monastery above this gate and held a magnificent zikr, chanting the name of God in mystical abandon, every Thursday night.

The guide also does not like my asking too many questions. He clearly has a job to do and is a man who likes to finish his job fast. He wants me to see the mosque quickly, before it is time for the Friday noon prayers. Actually, as I discover later, he is not a guide at all but more a member of a caretaker team.

I take off my shoes under one of the seven open arches of the Al-Aqsa Mosque—a medley of Crusader and Mamluk construction—and walk barefoot along the carpeted floor, from the entrance right up to the prayer niche, and from Çelebi's three-century-old descriptions I know this is three hundred paces. And he also counted the seventy large and small pillars 'of exquisite shape, of sumac-red and other colours... Each column is a jewel in itself, worth the "treasure of Egypt".' I look up to see the ancient beams of cypress wood and then into the elliptical dome, which Çelebi described as 'serene and unequalled on earth...the king of all domes around.' The pillars on the eastern side, those of the Carrara marble, are relatively new, said to have been donated by Mussolini in 1938.

It is not yet prayer time and men and women sit in small groups or pray singly and quietly. For the formal prayers the women will sit in the Dome beyond, and the mosque itself and the courtyard between it and the Dome will fill with rows of men.

Despite myself I search for the pulpit which I know is no longer there—the one carved out of cedar wood and brought by Saladin from Alleppo after he had cleansed the mosque of the presence of the Templar knights, knocked down the internal walls they had set up and uncovered the mihrab that they had bricked up. He had then ordered the pulpit to be brought from Damascus. Of it, Çelebi wrote: 'in order to show his skill, the accomplished master has made the pulpit as if it were the work of witchcraft.' Not too long ago it was destroyed in an act of vandalism when a radical Christian from Australia set the place on fire.

We make a quick foray into the underground mosque towards the eastern wall of the Haram. Schoolgirls are studying in its shaded coolness, leaning their uniformed backs against its ancient stone pillars. There are still holes in the pillars for the iron rings on which the Crusaders tied their horses; during their time, this place had been turned into a stable. Perhaps it is to these iron rings that Çelebi believes Solomon had tied up evil spirits. This is the Marwani mosque, named after Abdul al-Malik Marwan, the man who first started the construction of the fabled Dome of the Rock in AD 688 towards which we now walk, eyes blinking in the blazingly bright sun, reflected off the rough-hewn Herodian stones under our feet.

On the way, Nazeer points towards a medium-sized olive tree.

'My father likes to sit under that tree during his prayers. That is his place.'

Another tiny image of Sheikh Munir's life clicks into place.

The Dome of the Rock is not a mosque but a shrine, built to challenge the magnificence of Christian buildings in Jerusalem. It encloses the ancient rock that protruded from the flagstones of Herod's platform—the rock around which centre beliefs and legends of Jews, Christians and Muslims. This, it is said, is the place from where God took the dust to create Adam, the summit of the Biblical Mount Moriah where Abraham came to sacrifice his son, the foundation, or possibly the Holy of Holies of Solomon's Temple, the centre of the world, the entrance to the Garden of Eden, the place from where the Prophet ascended on his night journey to the heavens, the qibla of the Muslims for the first seventeen years of Islam; the blue colour of its Iznik tiles suggests infinity, the resplendent gold of its Dome represents knowledge.

An amazed Çelebi wrote: 'During these thirty-eight years whilst I travelled through seventeen countries, this site stands unique amongst the buildings I have seen, as if it were one of eight Paradises.' As was his wont, he immediately started measuring its dimensions, concluding its circumference to be three hundred paces. The variegated veined marble of its encasing walls rose to the height of three men.

Another indefatigable traveller, Ibn Battuta, too was deeply moved by this monument: 'This is one of the most fantastic of all buildings. Its queerness and perfection lie in its shape, though it has more than its fair share of other charms. It is so amazing it captivates the eye.' But Ibn Battuta did not see the amazing intricate tile work that Çelebi saw; it was put into place only by Suleiman the Magnificent in 1552. The resplendent Dome was not always like this. At least in the nineteenth century it was a dull lead colour, much like the dome of the Al-Aqsa. It was given a gold finish first in 1964 when gold coloured anodized aluminium sheets were put on it, but they did not prove to be watertight. In 1994, King Hussein of Jordan hired an Irish firm to do what is visible today. Copper and nickel were layered on to brass plates and the whole was then covered with a two-micron film of gold.

Inside is a carpeted landscape of impressive magnificence, of stained glass windows, decorated pillars, intricate unspoilt mosaics and ancient monolithic columns. In the centre, under the glorious double dome that seems to reach for the heavens, is the ancient rock. A short staircase leads to a grotto below the rock. One legend has it that when the Prophet ascended to the heavens, the rock followed him on his journey. It was then commanded by Gabriel to stay behind. Hence it remains hanging, unhinged from the earth, creating the grotto below it. Here pious pilgrims gather to pray at the prayer niches of the prophets. Here, too, it is believed the spirits of the dead gather twice a week to pray. This is the Well of Souls.

Outside the Dome, a number of shrines, prime among them the minbar of Qadi Burhanuddin, the Dome of the Chain, the el-Kas fountain, dot the wide open platform of the Haram. But the guide is chasing us on. Almost against his wish, we enter the office of the Servants of the Mosque. It is run by the Ansari family, not related to the family of Sheikh Munir, but a local Ansari family. Their ancestor came to the city with Caliph Omar and they have looked after the mosque—its visitors, its upkeep—for centuries. The Ansari representative inside greets us warmly and a cup of weak Arabic coffee is quickly offered. Not far from that office, behind a railing is the grave of Muhammad Ali al-Hindi, the leader of the Khilafat Movement and the one instrumental in sending Sheikh Nazir Ansari to Jerusalem. Buried in these hallowed precincts, the name of India attached to him for eternity.

The guide is grumpy now, mumbling under his breath. We have outlasted our welcome beyond any pretence of courtesy. I stop for a moment amidst young Palestinian boys kicking a soccer ball over the ancient flagstones and take a long, lingering look around.

The eye travels easily over the colonnaded porches along the extremities of the Haram. These porches housed madaris, ribai, zawiyat, libraries and fountains built during the Mamluk era for looking after the poor and the needy and for housing pilgrims. Here Sufis used to live and gather through the centuries, performing their exercises and praying within sight of the Dome. Çelebi describes the scene during the seventeenth century:

> All along the southern, western, and northern side of the Haram enclosures are porticoes with domes, resting over three hundred and sixty columns (and piers). All porticoes are lit every night by oil lamps. They become as bright as broad daylight. In these porticoes live dervishes from India, Sind, Balkh, Persia, and Kurds, Tartars, Moghuls, and Turks. They need by night no special candle lights, for [the oil lamps give so much light that] they can read the Quran [by that light], and recite the zikr and offer God the best prayers.

I turn to leave and then stop again. On an impulse, I ask Nazeer whether we can see the Indian Hospice from here.

'Of course,' he says. 'You can see the trees.'

I follow his finger pointing to the north. I can see, surprisingly near, rising over the walls and domes, the top of a Washingtonia palm tree. And I can imagine, through the clamour of the crashing centuries, Indian dervishes in these porticoes, and in the zawiya, spread out in different houses in the lanes of Bab Hutta, right up to Herod's Gate, which doesn't seem far at all.

We leave the Haram through the Bab al-Qattanin and enter the Suq al-Qattanin, or the Cotton Merchants Market. This commercial centre from which twenty-seven steps led up to the Haram platform was built by the Mamluk sultan Al-Nasir Muhammad in the early fourteenth century in immediate contact with the Haram wall, as was considered auspicious. He was the sultan who also commissioned the colonnaded porticoes on the northern and western borders of the Haram, restored the Aqsa dome and the Dome of the Rock. It was in this suq that foreign traders, including those from India, came to trade textiles, soap, leather and metalwork.

View of the old city from a rooftop with the Mount of Olives in the background

The Dome of the Rock

The Indian flag flutters proudly at the entrance of the Indian Hospice

الزاوية الهندية

Sheikh Munir in a meditative pose

The underground room (or chilla) where Baba Farid is believed to have meditated 800 years ago

An Israeli soldier watches a Palestinian woman climb up to the Indian Hospice Street

Father Jayaseelan, who could well be the first Indian priest at the Holy Sepulchre church in 2,000 years

Munther Fahmi in his bookshop at the American Colony

Al Wad street in the Muslim quarter on a Ramadan night

Sheikh Munir Ansari (left) with the author (centre) and son Nazeer Ansari

Orthodox Jews praying at the Western Wall

From left: the author, Wafa, Ikram, Avina Sarna, Najam, Nourjahan and Sheikh Munir

We stop at a small café, so small that its little stools are placed right in the bazaar. We order coffee and my mind goes back to a snippet I read somewhere. The qadi of Jerusalem issued an order in 1565 to extirpate and eliminate coffee houses from the hallowed places in Jerusalem. This order was in response to a complaint a certain Shaikh Nasiruddin made that the coffee houses that had been established at five places were the 'meeting place of rascals and ungodly people who day and night do not cease to act wickedly and mischievously, perniciously and refractorily', thus keeping the worshippers from pious devotion and divine worship.

I am glad that the qadi's order no longer holds. I wonder what the Old City would feel like without the cafés that are the heart of the crowded lanes, the throbbing sources of gossip and rumour, the gathering places of men bent over backgammon boards, their water pipes in one hand, a small cup of strong coffee, unsweetened and laced with cardamom before them, the coffee to which I already feel helplessly addicted.

15

'Bas, Love at First Sight'

There is no story that Sheikh Munir delighted in telling more than the one about Najam. The love of his life, perhaps the only regret of his life, the one after whom he named his eldest daughter. The mere mention of her name would take decades off his face and wreathe it in smiles. The eyes would begin to twinkle and his voice would acquire a gurgling resonance. Lifelong passions, I suppose, do these things. So I asked him to tell me the story more than once, not so much to get the facts but to see him in that mood.

'It was 1950,' he starts off one evening over home-made cake and tea. 'The war was over. My job with NAAFI was over. I was just, yaani, hanging around, not doing much. In those days a pilgrim came to stay with us here. He was a businessman called Hajji Abdul Latif Memon.

'One day he asked me, "O Munir, do you want to come to India?" I was of course ready in an instant but my father would not hear of it. "India? You 'majnoon' Munir," he said. "You have not even been to Amman and you want to go to India?"

'But I think for the first time, I disobeyed my father. I left with the hajji. I still had a British passport of the Mandate time. This was before I had got myself an Indian passport. We took off from the small airport near Qalandiya. It was a small plane with the, what is it called, wheel, fan…'

'Propeller?'

'Yes, yes, propeller. Very small plane. We went from here to Cairo. Then to Damascus, then Beirut. From there to Baghdad and then to Basra,' his flexed index finger sketches out a flight map across the evening sky as he talks. 'From Basra we took a ship to Kuwait and then another one to cross the Persian Gulf and reach Karachi.

'There I told the hajji—I need some time, maybe twenty-four hours or so. He said go, so I put the three suitcases that I was carrying for him in the customs and set off for Bahawalpur. My sisters—half-sisters—were there. My father's daughters from his Indian wife before he came to Palestine: Shakila and Naseema. They had moved to Pakistan after India's partition. My uncle Masud, Khwaja Masud Hasan Ansari, my father's brother, was in Multan.'

'Where was Najam?' I ask, unable to be patient.

'In Multan,' he smiles. 'She was my uncle's daughter. When I reached there, I met my uncle for the first time. I kissed his hand, he hugged me and all that. Then he called his children—Oye, come, idhar aao, your brother has come from Falastin, he said. He had two sons and four daughters. All the girls were veiled and they politely greeted me, "*Adaab arz hai, bhai sahib*." The youngest of them was called Najam. But I could hardly see her face behind the veil. Then they gave me a separate room to sleep in. I wasn't going to give up so easily. I waited for my uncle to leave the house for some work and I asked my aunt in Urdu to introduce me properly to my cousins: "*Chachi, woh hamari behnein kahan hai? Unse milwaiye*." She called them all into the room and I was introduced to them one by one.'

His face breaks into blushing smiles.

'Then Najam dropped her veil slowly and showed me her face.

A quarter of her face, then half and then full. *Bas, hubb bi'n-nazar ul awal.* It was what you call, love at first sight.'

'What did you do?'

'What could I do? I had to leave, but I knew I would come back. I completed the journey that I had set out for with the hajji, doing his business in Bombay and then in Ceylon. I returned to Jerusalem and went straight to my father. Before I had left for India, there had been some talk about my marriage. My mother had wanted me to marry a Palestinian girl but my father's preference was that I should marry an Indian girl; otherwise, he said, I would not be counted as his son. You see, after all I was his eldest son.

'So now I told him that I had met Najam and I wanted his permission to marry her. He wasn't very happy actually. He said that he had already planned that I should marry Najam's elder sister and had been meaning to talk to my uncle about that. But I was very clear. It had to be Najam. So he agreed. He gave me some money, a gold bangle and a ring and said, "Yalla, go then." So off I was to India again, again with the same Hajji Memon. I completed the business with him and again went to Multan.'

'Were they expecting you to return?'

'Yes, of course. My father had already written to my uncle to formalize my marriage with Najam. But somehow my uncle did not take that step. I was allowed to stay and treated very well, but the marriage was not mentioned. Once in a while I would try to push him by saying—"*Chacha ji, woh hamari shaadi Najam ke sath?*" (What about my marriage with Najam?) He would say, "Yes, yes, what's the hurry, wait." I spent a long time there, about four months. Sometimes I would stay with my uncle and at other times I would go away to Bahawalpur to my half-sisters.'

'And all this time, did you talk to her, get to know her at all?'

'Oh yes, of course. One of my half-sisters was married to a deputy inspector of schools. He had a car. Sometimes he would come to Multan and leave the car for me and go back by train. I would then take Najam and her sisters in the car to picnic in the garden by the canal. I was quite desperate to marry her but I wanted to do it the right way. I was so desperate that my half-sisters even told me that they would get Najam to Bahawalpur and I could marry her and take her away to Jerusalem even if my uncle did not agree. But I did not want that. After all, my father was still alive. What would he say? He would say you were to marry her, not to steal her...yes, I was not "bahadur".'

He falls silent, thinking what his life would have been if he had indeed defied his uncle and brought Najam to Jerusalem anyway. When he looks up, his eyes are distant, his voice quieter. The laughter has turned to a sad, regretful smile.

'Finally, after four months, my uncle said, "Munir, I have decided. I will go with you to Falastin." I knew this was a disaster. I tried to tell him that he should let me marry Najam and then we could all visit Jerusalem, but he would have none of it. "I haven't seen my brother for twenty years. I will go with you to Bait ul-Maqdis and we will then see about the marriage." When Najam learnt about this, she cried a lot. She said, "Munir, now it will never happen. He will go with you to Falastin and see how you live, how free you all are there and he will never agree to my going there."

'That is exactly what happened. When my uncle came here my father was in his last days and was mostly in bed. And all the women and girls in the house were around him and mixing freely. My sisters were wearing skirts and going around without veils. My uncle saw all this and probably made up his mind there and then that he did not want his daughter to live in such a free atmosphere. I did tell my father that he should talk to his brother about the marriage. From his reply, I could surmise that he had probably already broached the subject. He told me in Arabic—"If this happens, Munir, then it is good and if it does not happen, then it is better than good."

'My father died when my uncle was on his return journey to Multan. When he reached back there was a telegram waiting for him telling him of his brother's death. After the mourning period was over, I prevailed upon my stepmother, Mariam, to write to my uncle. She did, saying that his brother was no more, that this was Allah's wish and that now he should come and take over the hospice and be the head of the family. Of course this was all my idea as I was still hoping that this way I could marry Najam.'

'Did he respond?' I ask.

'Yes, he did reply. He said that his brother had lived his life in Palestine and that had been his destiny. But this was not his destiny and he could not come to the hospice. He also added that he could not marry his daughter Najam to Munir. Bas, that was the end of the story.'

'Was it really the end?' I persist. 'I seem to remember that you had mentioned once that you had met her again.'

'Yes, I met her again more than twenty years later when I visited her. She had had a very difficult life. Her sister died and her father married her off to the same man. He already had five children. Then she had five more with him. And he died. So when I met her she was already a widow with ten children. She cried and shouted all the time during the two hours we were with her, and I realized that the visit was a big mistake. In front of her children, she kept saying that she would never be able to forgive her father for not allowing her to marry this Munir and instead pawning her off to a man with five children. It was sad but I have never forgotten her. I named my first daughter after her...then I tried to marry her daughter Tehmina to Nazeer. I brought her photograph with me and showed it to Nazeer. Tehmina means valuable, but he said, "Baba, this is the twentieth century, we cannot marry like this." So that was the real end of the Najam story.'

Quietly we let the memory go to sleep. Then Nazeer makes a brave attempt to bring the cheer back to the conversation. He puts an arm around his wife's shoulder and says, 'If I would have married this Tehmina, how could I have got my beloved Wafa?' Wafa shrugs him off with an imperious jerk and the smiles come back slowly.

'But you did get married rather quickly to Ikram after that; tell us how it happened,' I grasp at the changed mood.

'Not immediately,' he smiles and decides to carry on with his talk, putting away Najam to that corner of his heart where she seems to live all the time. 'After my father died and I had been sheikh of the hospice for about a year, my mother and Mariam came up with an idea. There was a girl in a family in Nablus who they thought would be suitable for me. I was reluctant to go and see her as I did not want a rejection. But finally we took some gifts and went. She did not have a father, only a brother. When the proposal was put to the brother, he dilly-dallied, saying his sister was only seventeen and in school. He wanted her to study another two or three years. I had not expected that; I had thought they would jump at the idea and welcome me with open arms into the family. The same night I made Mariam and my mother pack their things and immediately we returned to Jerusalem.

'Then I took matters in my hand. I told my mother and Mariam that there are three girls in the families that we know—Ikram, Fauziya and one other one. I said I leave the choice from among these three to you. They agreed on Ikram. She was also related to my grandmother's family. I immediately called up her brother. He was a senior functionary in the governor's office and I asked to see him in his office. As soon as I sat in his office I did not waste any words. I told him that I had come to ask for the hand of his sister Ikram. He agreed the same minute. I told him that he should ask her, he should ask his father. But he said there is no need, I have given you my word.'

'My mother too had been given six names and she too had picked the name of Munir. You see, it was written,' adds Najam.

'They wanted to perform the marriage after six months. I asked why. They said they needed time to make the dress and so on. I said there is no need to wait. I had money those days. We had a large number of pilgrims in the one year that I had been sheikh, so I gave about 250 Jordanian dinars as "mehr" and we got married straightaway.'

Nazeer has pulled out a wedding photo. A black-and-white photo but we know Ikram's dress was blue; that was how Munir wanted it. And he himself wore a handsome suit and white leather shoes. And immediately they left on a whirlwind honeymoon—Jericho, Amman, Beirut, Alexandria, Cairo and finally Gaza. It was an adventure: Ikram did not have time to get a passport made and she travelled on the one that belonged to her sister-in-law Hind. Nobody much cared those days. The British Mandate passport did not have photographs of Muslim women; they were simply described as 'purdah nashin', or in purdah. More than once they had a narrow escape when they ran into people they knew and had to answer how the Indian-looking Hind had suddenly turned into this fair and blonde Palestinian girl.

'And he took his stepmother along with him on his honeymoon,' Nazeer reveals.

'Why?'

'Because I wanted to go and see the Gaza property that belonged to the hospice. Mariam had been there with my father and they knew her. I had to take her with me. We waited twenty-one days in Egypt to get a permit to get into Gaza.'

'And what were the sleeping arrangements?'

'We used to take one room and draw a curtain in the middle.'

16

The Burden of a Father's Turban

In conversation after conversation, I noticed a strong reluctance on the part of Sheikh Munir to criticize his stepmother. He would rather leave a pretty picture about the past, a picture in which everyone lived together as a happy large family of Sheikh Nazir Ansari, various wives in separate quarters, children playing happily together, a model of coexistence. A coexistence that led to peaceful succession after Sheikh Nazir's death and continued to prevail in the hospice until Mariam's departure in 1967. But as we got to know each other better and he became freer with his thoughts and words, the pain that he carried somewhere in his heart began to rise to the surface. Once in a while, the pretty picture would dissolve into real human beings.

'It was in 1947 that my father allowed us to return to the hospice,' Sheikh Munir says with a wan smile on his face, 'after I told him that my sisters are now grown-up. As I told you we had to sign an agreement that we would not trouble my stepmother or her children. So we stayed in one room in the front wing of the hospice. It's the room that forms part of Nazeer's house now. My mother, my maternal grandmother, I and my four sisters—Hind, Leyla, Amina and Fatima—all in that one room. It was like I had won a war that day. To bring back my mother and sisters with my stepmother living in the house—it was quite incredible. Hind had moved in earlier with my father. My father had allowed her and of course it was more comfortable for her in the hospice where there were beds and electricity; outside, there was nothing of that kind. She cooked for him and Mariam. In fact we would take flour from her for our bread. Whenever it finished one of us would come with a basin to ask for more. Hind would have to take orders from Mariam and give us two or three days of ration every time. We wondered why we could not get a larger quantity but no, that was what Mariam decided. Actually Mariam wanted all the children to move in with my father and leave my mother alone outside. That would have finished my mother; fortunately, that did not happen.'

He goes quiet whenever he thinks of that time. It could not have been easy, to be the eldest son of his father and yet have to beg for what was clearly his by right.

One day he goes further.

'There was another incident,' he begins and then falls silent again for a long time, debating with himself whether he should relate that incident at all. Finally, having started the thought, he decides to carry on.

'When we were still outside the hospice, I came here one day. In fact I used to come here every day, to see my father, to work with the soldiers in the Chhota Club. I must have been about sixteen years old. The war was still on, the soldiers were still around. Here, in this courtyard, were the offices of the director of the leave camp, the superintendent and so on. There were tents outside for the kitchens, and the barracks—the Travancore and Delhi wings—had been built. My father used to stay upstairs. I went up and I was met by Hind. She took me aside.

'"Do you know what is cooking here, Munir?"

'"What?" I asked.

'"One of these dervishes, these hajjis who stay here, he is causing trouble for you."

'"Who? Which one?"

'"That Mahboub," she whispered.

'"What is he up to?"

'"He brought a bomb, a hand grenade, to Baba and he said that you had given it to him to throw it at the zawiya."

'I was very angry; I could not believe what was happening. I went straight to that hajji. I caught him and beat him up. Then I told him that I would do more damage to him if he did not tell me the truth. Finally, he cracked and spilt the beans. He said that a man from the Afghan Hospice had put him up to telling that story to my father. I caught him by his neck and took him up to my father's room. Mariam was sitting there with my father. Hind was in the kitchen.

'"Come on, tell the truth now," I told the hajji.

'He stood quietly and wouldn't say anything. But I was not going to give up. So I gave him a few hard slaps right there in my father's room. I had never behaved like that in front of my father. In fact he was so shocked with my behaviour he shouted in Urdu: *"Oye badmash, kya karta hai?"*

'"I will do worse," I said, "unless the man tells the truth in front of you."

'Finally, the man admitted that he had lied and that someone had put him up to try and do damage to my relationship with my father.'

'My father died in 1951. His last few months had been spent in bed. He died with all of us around him, soon after my uncle, Najam's father, had left for his home.'

I have seen the photograph in the old albums that must surely be the last of Sheikh Munir's father. It was taken one month before he died. He is lying on his deathbed, his face gaunt and bony, the children all gathered around him. Munir is right behind him, handsome in a tweed jacket, his wavy hair neatly combed. Mariam stands next to him with her hand touching the head of the old dying man; Mussarra, the Palestinian wife and Munir's mother, is not in the photograph. But the children are, as is Munir's uncle Masud, in a recently acquired suit and tasselled tarboosh.

'My father had lived for nearly three decades in Palestine when he died. He should have been buried here, within the hospice,' Munir was speaking. 'That is a tradition here, in many of the zawiyat: the sheikhs are buried inside the premises. The sheikh of Naqshbandi tariqa, Sheikh Bukhari, who was a very famous and wise man, the most respected of all sheikhs of my father's time, is buried inside the Uzbek Hospice. Here, too, you have seen that we have two graves inside the hospice. Probably these are graves of some earlier sheikhs. But we could not do that with my father. When he died, Mariam was not in favour of burying him in the hospice. She said she has to live here, work here and it would pain her to see the grave of her husband all the time. So we buried my father in the cemetery outside Herod's Gate, the cemetery of Bab al-Zahira.'

Later, on a Saturday, Nazeer guides me to the cemetery that opens out on Salahdin Street. There are no municipal restraints on Saturday and the whole street will soon become a bazaar of pavement sellers. Already several Palestinian women have set out their baskets of grapes.

'These are from Hebron,' Nazeer points out. 'They are smaller and sweeter than the Israeli ones.'

We enter the green gate of the cemetery; www.alqudstombs.com—announces the board that stretches over it.

'There are three cemeteries in Jerusalem—this one, the one near the wall of the Haram and the one in Mamilla. This one was mostly for old Jerusalem families.'

A few steps and then a hill rises gently. Dry, stony graves cover every bit of the hill.

'They have recently cleaned it up. The organization that looks after these cemeteries got some donations. All these tiles are new, so is this shelter where the families of those being buried wait and accept condolences. Come, first we will see my grandmother.'

We turn to the left and not too far away is a grave where lies Mussarra, the mother of Sheikh Munir. She died, as the gravestone says, on 7 June 1967. Along with her is buried her daughter Amina who died on the same day. Both were killed in the Israeli shelling of the Indian Hospice. Three years ago, the tomb was opened to add Layla, another of Munir's sisters.

We climb to the top of the hill. But before that at least three people come and ask us our purpose. Nazeer tells them who he is, quelling their suspicion. I cannot help thinking again how suspicious everyone is of anybody who is not known, even if they are walking around in a cemetery.

Sheikh Nazir Ansari's grave is a high one in a style that seems to have been popular at that time. The inscription on the stone has been painted in black not too long ago. It tells the visitor that this is the grave of Sheikh Nazir Ansari of the Indian Hospice who was also the mutawalli of the waqf, that he was born in Saharanpur in India and died in Jerusalem in 1951. A thorny bush is beginning to grow near the grave.

'We got it cleaned up but this bush comes back. I will send Abu Ziad to clean it again.'

'And you became sheikh of the hospice straightaway?'

Sheikh Munir laughs.

'I did and I didn't.'

Then he laughs again at my perplexed expression. It's nice

to see him laugh. His spectacles begin to shine and his face loses years in a moment.

'After the burial, there was mourning for three days. All the sheikhs, the mukhtars and the ordinary people came to the hospice and condoled with us. My father was known as Sheikh Ansari al-Hindi all over the city. He used to say that I have lived so long here but they still call me al-Hindi. When all the sheikhs were sitting in the reception room upstairs, I was called by Sheikh Bukhari.

'"Go get your father's turban," he told me.

'I went to my father's bedroom and got his turban from Mariam. Then Sheikh Bukhari spoke to the gathering. He talked about my father and his life and work. Then he said that the old Sheikh Ansari had lived his life and was now with Allah. But life must go on and there was need for the Zawiya al-Hindiya to get a new sheikh. He made me wear my father's turban and then said that I, Munir Mohammad Ansari, would be the new sheikh. They all hugged me and congratulated me and that was that.'

'That seems to have been pretty simple and straightforward,' I commented.

'It wasn't, actually. Of course the sheikhs had decided I was the sheikh but it was not yet formal. I had to be taken to the sharia court and made the mutawalli of the waqf. I also had to see if Mariam, who was very powerful in the hospice, accepted it. After all, she and her children were all part of my family, the family of my father. She wanted to make her son Ahmad the sheikh and mutawalli of the zawiya. But at that time he was only about fourteen. That was the problem. There used to be a tailor, a man by the name of Sayeed, living at the hospice those days. It was rumoured that Mariam would marry Sayeed and the two of them would look after the affairs of the hospice until Ahmad came of age and could officially take over.

'I really had no one to go to for advice except one man. He

was a qadi, Sheikh Assad el-Imam, whom I had made my guru. He used to live on the Haram. I discussed the matter with him and then laid out my plan. I went and told Mariam: "It is true that you came here and married my father, you took the place of my mother. You and your children stayed here while we could not stay here and had to live in difficult circumstances outside the hospice. After a long time I managed to bring my mother and sisters back here. Now I am the sheikh of the hospice as the eldest son of my father. You and your children can stay here and, if you so decide, I will look after everybody. But I cannot keep any new husband here. If you want to marry this man then you and your children have to go. And please understand, I am the sheikh and this is not a temporary arrangement until Ahmad becomes an adult." She saw the logic of what I was saying and gave up her plans of marrying the tailor if she ever had them and we all began to live together.'

Things don't change that much down the centuries. For one, people continue to fight about more or less the same things.

One document that Nazeer has found dates back to the year AH 1092 or AD 1681. It is a judgement of the sharia judge of the time, Maulana Mohammed Effendi bin Abdul Baqi (May his excellence endure forever, as the document says). The case before him is a dispute between one Abdul Aziz al-Hindi and Bahai-ud-din, the sheikh of the Multan Indians. Abdul Aziz had produced a decree of a year earlier, issued by the Ottoman sultan stating that he had been appointed sheikh of the Indian Hospice by Mahmoud Shahabuddin. Bahai-ud-din took the position that the sheikh of the hospice could only be a person the Indians approve of and the waqf regulations demand that the sheikh should be a man of religiosity. Bahai-ud-din produced a document showing that he had been appointed the sheikh by the sharia judge of Jerusalem two years earlier on account of his religiosity and suitability. The judge then asked Abdul Aziz if the person who gave him the document had ever acted before in the matter of the hospice, to which Abdul Aziz responded that he was not aware. Then a group of Indian and other Muslims came to the maulana and testified that Sheikh Bahai-ud-din was a man of religiosity and virtue and was the only one who was suitable to be the sheikh. The other man Abdul Aziz was in fact a tramp, an untrustworthy person and not someone who could be trusted with the belongings of the hospice. The maulana ruled in favour of Bahai-ud-din as sheikh. The order was witnessed by as many as eight sheikhs.

That document, and similar others, helps me understand many things. I know for sure now that the tradition of an Indian being in charge of this hospice did not start with Sheikh Nazir Ansari of Saharanpur; several others, centuries before, had names suffixed with 'al-Hindi' or 'Dehlvi', indicating their Indian roots. Several of us have walked these narrow lanes for centuries. That is why Sheikh Nazir could not shed off his Indianness after three decades and that is why I am chased by snatches of Hindi songs and that is why a toothless, wizened old lady with a nose ring tugged at my sleeve near the ribat of the Africans and asked me if I knew Amitabh Bachchan. I also learn what it takes to be a sheikh, why Shiekh Munir's father preferred to live a life of material modesty and why it is important that his son Nazer, destined to be the next sheikh, has the advantage of an education from Al-Azhar University in Cairo. Most important, it helps me understand why Munir himself has always conducted himself, despite all odds, in a manner that generates respect. I look at him as he sits, a man past eighty, proud, undefeated, a true sheikh. He seems to have lived by the motto that is on his writing desk: *'Emal lidunyak kaanak tayesh abadan wa emal laakaratak kaanak tamout gadan'* or 'Work for your earthly life as if you would live forever, work for your end as if you would die tomorrow.'

It's nearing lunchtime and I have made no serious move to

leave. I am lost in the documents. I do not even notice that the ladies—Najam and her mother—have vanished. Najam reappears in a while, while we are still poring over the documents in the small office room.

'Lunch is ready,' she announces, and I realize that it is no use now trying to sound polite. I have already put them out.

We are not eating in the courtyard of the hospice where we often drink tea, nor in the little garden with the fountain, outside the sheikh's living quarters. Instead I am led inside to the family dining room, where I have never been before. It's a warm and friendly room, a room with its walls full of family photographs, a room made cosier by an open kitchen. The main dish too is new for me: carrots stuffed with meat and cooked in gravy.

'My mother's stuffed carrots are the best,' Nazeer digs in.

There is also a last minute dish, a special concession to this guest who wouldn't leave: scrambled eggs and potatoes.

'This is what every housewife makes when she is very tired,' Najam explains helpfully.

And to finish off, there are sweet oranges from Jericho and Arabic coffee made just right—'nus-nus' or fifty-fifty on the sugar.

17

An Evening of Coincidence

I walk into Munther's shop. He is about to dip a piece of pita into a dish of hummus. Seeing me he stops and attempts to get up, slightly embarrassed.

'That's early for dinner?'

'Early? For me it's too late! Oh God, what would I do without my mother? You know, she sends my food in a taxi.'

He is putting on a brave face but I can see his heart in not in it. His smile is forced, there is no jauntiness to his walk. Even the straw hat at that rakish angle, to which I have so got used to, is missing.

'I have a problem,' he says. 'I need to get someone to give me a visa. This time I came they said it was the last time I would be allowed in on a tourist visa. I have to do something. But I don't know where to start… I mean I am a Palestinian, this is my land and I can't get a visa!'

We sit on a small table in the veranda outside his shop and order Arabic coffee. A large poster showing a bus travelling through a desert with silhouettes of palm trees and a mosque leans against the wall behind him. It is a poster commemorating the Desert Mail service, once run by the Nairn Transport Company. We begin to talk about it.

'There was a railway too,' says Munther. 'My grandfather came from Egypt to work on the railway at Haifa. He settled down in Akko. Unfortunately the war—the First War—started and the railway was never completed. You can still see the rails near the Lebanese border.'

But the Desert Mail consisted of American vehicles that took people and mail from Haifa to Damascus, Beirut, Baghdad, even India.

'The name Nairn?' I ask. 'It's almost Indian. We have Narayan.'

'Mr Nairn is walking towards us,' says Munther and I turn to meet a Scotsman of medium height and middle age, neatly turned out in a blazer. He is a co-owner of the American Colony Hotel, now settled in Inverness. He used to work in the hotel in the seventies. That explains his easy familiarity with the surroundings.

'It was a great service, the Desert Mail,' he explains as he joins us. 'They used sturdy American vehicles. It was the best way to get your mail those days. I wish I could tell you that the Desert Mail belonged to my family. That would be neat. The service belonged to a Scottish family that migrated to New Zealand. That I have the same name, I part own this place and I am here today as you speak of it—it's all just a coincidence.'

But it's the kind of coincidence that doesn't seem strange at the American Colony, or in Jerusalem.

Reaching the American Colony to meet Sheikh Munir's family for tea had not been easy that midsummer day. The Haredim were out in their thousands in Jerusalem. They were protesting the high court ruling against the discrimination that keeps Sephardi girls out of Orthodox Jewish schools, run and attended almost exclusively by the Ashkenazis. About thirty-five fathers who refused to send their Ashkenazi girls to these schools in protest were being taken to prison. And the protestors, in their black suits and fedora hats, with their blonde ringlets and beards, were out in strength to fete these men as heroes, comparing the high court to the Pharoah and to Antioch in its harshness to the Jews. The streets were closed, the traffic disrupted. But finally the Haredim began to return home and even the policemen and women on duty took a break, sitting on the pavement in the shadow of a bus and opening cans of soda.

But Sheikh Munir and his family are soon there and we head towards the garden bar, crowded with sofas and chairs. Reluctant to miss the gathering, Munther says that he will shut his shop and join us.

Sheikh Munir asks the portly Arab headwaiter for tea.

But they don't serve tea here. This, after all, is a bar.

'But I am a Muslim,' says the sheikh. 'I do not drink. What should I do?'

'Fresh juice? Or a fruit cocktail.'

Sheikh Munir agrees but clearly he is upset. He is even more upset when I tell the waiter that I will pay the bill.

'But why? We invited you.'

'Yes, Sheikh Sahib, but I cannot allow you to pay for my alcohol.'

We compromise with the promise that I will have lunch the following week at the hospice with him. Munther has joined us now. He wants to visit the hospice. As a child, he has lived only 'two blocks away', as he says, from the hospice; he has played den on the steps that lead down to Herod's Gate. His father, it turns out, was the principal of the same school where Sheikh Munir's wife has taught all her life. It's a small world, we all agree, as the drinks come. Someone orders a shandy, Munther says he has never heard of a shandy.

Sheikh Munir is again grumpy.

'I want to complain to someone. How can they decide what I should drink? As a Jerusalemite, I should be free to drink what I want.'

From the small mosque behind the hotel, the muezzin begins to call for the Asr prayers.

'He doesn't have a nice voice,' is Najam's verdict. 'Some have very nice voices, this one doesn't.'

There is a fragment that I have read in the diaries of Wasif Jawhariyyeh, the oud player and chronicler from the early twentieth century, that comes to mind at that remark. Wasif recalls how his father, Jiryis, who was the mukhtar of the Eastern Orthodox community in the Old City, once led a delegation to the awqaf department to request the replacement of a local imam whose voice they could not stand. The official questioned the credibility of Jiryis as a Christian to ask for the replacement of an imam but nevertheless explained that the muezzin was a poor orphan with a large family to support. Upon this, Jiryis suggested that the particular muezzin be relocated to the mosque behind the American Colony, where fewer people would have to listen to him. So outrageous was the request that it was actually acceded to. That must have been nearly a hundred years ago. Perhaps today's muezzin, whose voice so grated on Najam's ears, belonged to the same family.

It's an evening when one coincidence comes quickly on the heels of another.

As soon as the call for prayer stops, there are sudden fireworks in the sky. Sheikh Munir sees my look of surprise and smiles softly.

'East Jerusalem,' he says, as if that were explanation enough.

'Any occasion?'

'No,' Munther steps in, 'they do it all the time. It's very dangerous.'

18

A Passing Fancy in Dark Glasses

When Sheikh Munir inherited the hospice in 1951—he was eventually taken to the sharia court by the elder sheikhs and a proper certificate was issued declaring him to be the mutawalli, of the waqf of the Indian zawiya—it was in a different city than the one in which his father had lived.

The war of 1948 had divided Jerusalem between Jordan and the new state of Israel. The inhabitants of the Jewish quarter in the Old City had been expelled to West Jerusalem, and the Arab residents of the West had lost their homes. King Abdallah of Jordan was crowned King of Jerusalem by the Coptic bishop—and ironically, it was in Jerusalem that he was assassinated—and East Jerusalem as well as the West Bank of the Jordan river were declared Jordanian territory. Jordan-controlled Jerusalem, which contained the Old City, was different. In the words of Sari Nusseibeh:

> Gone were the English and Arab aristocrats, the free-wheeling parvenus, middle-class tradesmen, and the demimonde catering to soldiers; gone were the bohemians, servants, and British clerks; gone too were the rich blend of cultures—the bishops, Muslim clerics, and black-bearded rabbis crowding the same streets. What was left was a tired provincial city with barbed wire snaking through its

> center, and much of its political life drained off to the desert capital of Amman.

And Amos Oz would later describe thus the other side of the barbed wire:

> High concrete walls were erected along the line, to block streets that were half in Israeli Jerusalem and half in Arab Jerusalem. Here and there corrugated iron barriers were put up to conceal passers-by in West Jerusalem from the view of the snipers on the rooftops of the eastern part of the city. A fortified strip of barbed wire, minefields, firing positions and observation posts crossed the whole city, enclosing the Israeli section to the north, east and south. Only the west was left open, and a single winding road linked Jerusalem to Tel Aviv and the rest of the new state… Sometimes we were woken up in the early hours by machine-gun salvoes from the direction of the armistice line, a mile or so from where we lived, or the wailing of the muezzin on the other side of the new border: like a hair-raising lament the howl of his prayer penetrated our sleep.

Sheikh Munir does not have too many memories to share of the war of 1948. His stories revolve more around the Second World War days and the Indian soldiers in the hospice and then of the days of the early fifties, of his travels to find Najam, of his father's death, of his assumption of the office of the sheikh. But one day, when he looks through his papers, an old bank passbook comes out. Actually it's not from a bank but from the Palestinian post office. Saving account number 2884 opened on 3 September 1944. The passbook carries a dire warning on its cover: 'Keep this book in a safe place. Its loss may cause you trouble.' There are many entries, deposits and withdrawals of small sums, presumably squirrelled away by the young Munir from his early earnings at NAAFI. And then there is the last entry of withdrawal of seventy-four Palestinian pounds on 31 January 1948.

'I went to withdraw the money. War was breaking out. For the first time I saw two people behind the counter—an Arab and a Jew. They asked me: "Why do you want the money?" I want to buy a gun, I told them, don't you know we are going to have a war? But I did not buy a gun. I bought rice and sugar and other things and carried them away to Jericho to get through the months with my mother and sisters.'

In those difficult years, when East Jerusalem lived in the uneasy embrace of the Jordanians, suffering the burden of refugees, war damage and deteriorating conditions, the Indian Hospice could not have remained untouched.

While seeking assistance to maintain the hospice, Sheikh Nazir wrote in a letter to the Indian embassy in Cairo in November 1950:

> On account of the disturbances in Palestine, the Hospice was fully occupied by refugees & owing to the damage resulted to the Hospice from that, I wrote to the British Consul General at Jerusalem on the subject & unfortunately I discovered that most of the papers, registers, and furniture were stolen & destroyed by the refugees. I therefore regret to say that I am unable to give the number of visitors but able to give a rough number of visitors during the months of September & October, 1950. I beg to add that during the second Great War & for a period of nearly seven years the Hospice was occupied by the Indian Army and also two years after the war on account of Palestine trouble no visitors arrived. Visitors restarted to come from last year…

In another letter of the same year, he stresses that immediate repairs are needed 'in order to save from demolition the Travancore Wing, built during the Second World War and damaged during the Palestine conflict also, and many other premises... [T]he Hospice is without electric current, without a good sanitary installation and without also telephone.' Things must have deteriorated during the war; otherwise I have seen old letterheads, as far back as 1929, showing the telegram address of the hospice as Darul Aman and Hindustan and the telephone number as 755.

He points out that the 'actual income of the Indian Hospice is insignificant as I do not receive many pilgrims due to the actual world situation. Apart [from] that, the pilgrims visiting these places are not entitled to pay fees unless they make offers or gifts... This Hospice is the refuge of all Indians living in this country and of those coming from abroad including the diplomatic corps who prefer to come to us rather than go to hotels.'

One of the earliest travellers to visit the hospice after the disturbances of those years must have been Abu Al-Hasan Ali Al Hasni Al Nadawi, Islamic historian, scholar and author of more than fifty books. In his travelogue describing his journey of 1951, he writes:

> We stopped near Bab al Zahra and headed to the Indian hospice, where we kept our luggage in a room. We prayed Al Maghreb and headed to Al Masjid Al Aqsa, guided by one of the servants of the hospice. It was dark and the lights were dim. We couldn't figure out the landmarks well, passed by the Dome of the Rock and entered the southern Masjid known now as Al Aqsa masjid, in spite of the fact that everything within the wall is the Masjid al Aqsa, blessed by Allah.

Al Nadawi also records his awe at visiting the grave of Maulana

Muhammad Ali of the Khilafat Movement in the corridors that surround the Dome of the Rock.

Gradually but surely, the lot of the city began to improve. Al-Aqsa Mosque was restored in 1953 and new schools and hospitals were built by the Muslim Charitable Society. New homes began to come up for refugees and a new commercial district, the crowded district through which Salahdin Street runs to the American Colony, was established. The tourism industry developed rapidly and several modern hotels sprouted in East Jerusalem. Nusseibeh records this optimism:

> Jerusalem had recovered much of the life it had lost in 1948. As it had done time and time again throughout the ages, it had reasserted its role as the world capital of religious pilgrimage. The Jewish half was closed off by a wall. But since nearly all of the ancient sites were located in our half, tourists flooded in. Pope Paul VI's historic visit in 1964 sparked a speculative building boom. With the Zionist threat gone, centuries-old patterns reasserted themselves, and the old noble families were back on their feet. The Husseinis, Nashashibis, the Islamic scholars, and the Christian bishops now set the tone for the city. If you could ignore No Man's land and the refugee camps, it was as if nothing had ever happened.

Among the tourists that began to flood to this boomtown were the large numbers of pilgrims coming from India.

'Those were really the golden years for the hospice,' says Sheikh Munir, 'from 1952 to 1967 when the place was full of spirit, full of joy, full of pilgrims all the time. We all lived like one large family: Mariam and her children lived upstairs, I lived with Ikram and the children in this room in the courtyard, my mother and sisters lived in the front rooms.

'I used to take care of the place and Mariam would work as a tour guide; we made a very good team. She was very energetic and popular. Busloads of pilgrims would arrive and Mariam would wear her burqa and step out with them. One day she would spend with them in Jerusalem, the second day she would take them to Bethlehem and Hebron and the third day she would show them the Dead Sea, Nabi Musa and so on. She was tireless. This room where we now have the photographs and the visitor's book was my office. I used to sit here every day and do my bookkeeping and register all the visitors to the hospice, write down their passport numbers and so on.'

'So it did work well, with Mariam and her children and all of you?'

'It worked very well,' is Munir's genuine reaction. 'Actually she was very fond of me. In some ways, she was closer to me than my real mother. My sisters used to get angry at me when I said this, but it was true. Sometimes she used to tell her own children in Urdu—whenever she spoke to them it would be in Urdu—"All of you on one side and Munir alone on the other." In other words, that I was equal to all of them.'

'Tell me about her children.'

'She and my father had six children. The eldest was Ahmad who was born in 1938 and till recently he worked in the Indian embassy in Beirut. Then there were three other sons—Mahmoud, Hamid and Hassanein. There were two girls too—Suraya and Sarwar. I did not study in a university myself but I made sure that Mariam's boys studied. Ahmad and Mahmoud studied in Cairo, Hamid in Delhi and Hassanein in the US. One became an engineer, another a professor and a third an aviation engineer. The youngest sister Sarwar was ill and nobody could pay for her treatment. She too lived here with us until she died in the early seventies, young and unmarried. I believe I was true to my word to Mariam that I would look after them.'

He stops but seems to want to go on. I remain quiet, hoping that none of the family members will break his thought with some light-hearted remark. I know him well enough now to realize that he is probably debating with himself, to talk about some person, some incident or not. The moment holds and he starts speaking, with a glance at his wife.

'There was once a woman visitor during those years. From India. She came to me in that room where I used to make the lists of the visitors. She was carrying several passports with her. She sat down and handed them over to me. I looked at her. She was wearing a kurta-pyjama and a headscarf and dark glasses. Clearly she was not of the same class as the other seven people she was travelling with. They seemed poor and were staying in the free room of the hospice but she seemed well off. She took off her scarf and her dark glasses and I was swept off my feet. She was a real Indian beauty with the most beautiful eyes. I looked at her passport carefully. Her name was Yasmeen, she was about thirty-five and she was the wife of a senior Indian army officer.

'"I could not resist asking her—What are you doing with these people? You seem to be different. You are the wife of an army officer.

'"I am now divorced," she said.

'Anyhow I gave her a separate room where she began to stay. She asked me to take her to the mosque and other places. She did not want to go with Mariam. I said, chalo, so I took her to the Al-Aqsa where she prayed. Then I put her in my car—I used to have an Austin those days—and took her to the Dead Sea, Nabi Musa and so on. She talked to me a lot on the way. She asked me if I was married. I said yes, I am married and I have five children.'

He looks at his wife. She is quiet but her lips are pursed.

'I was late in returning. My wife was worried. She probably

thought that I had spent some time with Yasmeen and was angry about it. When we came back from the tour she scolded Yasmeen, accusing her of all sorts of things.'

There are smiles all around now and I am not sure how much of this story has been heard by any of his children before.

'My father was very handsome,' says one of his daughters.

'What do you mean, was?' cuts in the other. 'He still is.'

'Anyhow she went away to perform her hajj. From there she wrote me a long letter. She said that she had prayed for me during her "tawwaf". She told me that I had done a very wrong thing by marrying an Arab woman but there was still time. She was willing to come and live with me and be my wife. She wrote twice or thrice after that but I did not follow up. I did not want to get into the problems that my father had got into. I did not mind chatting with people like her in Urdu and all that, but that was all.'

We have been sitting in the small garden courtyard in front of the sheikh's house. Above us is a tall towering palm reaching into the blue sky; it is the Washingtonia that I could see from the Dome of the Rock. Beside it is a spreading olive tree.

'I planted both these in 1950,' he says with pride in his voice. 'This is the only olive tree in the Old City which produces black olives, except the trees around the Al-Aqsa Mosque.'

Maybe it is the torpor induced by the food, or the memory of the days in which he planted those trees, or the talk of the golden days of the hospice but he falls into a mellow, sad mood. A deep sense of mortality seems to overcome him.

'I have spent my whole life here. I have been head of the hospice, the sheikh, for nearly sixty years, and I have tried to do my best for it, to protect it. After me it is up to my family. We pray five times and each time we are to thank God for what he has given us. I think that even if I thank God fifty times a day it will not be enough for what he gave me. My life was very difficult, very complicated but I came on top… When I walk to the mosque people in the streets respect me… I take my grandson with me, I lean on him; when people see us they tell my grandson Amir, take care of your grandfather, he is a very special man.'

All of us around the table know that this is not the time for a flippant remark. And a few minutes later, Nazeer walks me out and we pause near the fruit vendors in the archway of Herod's Gate.

'He has been like this recently,' he says of his father's mood. 'My elder brother, Nazer, came after many years recently from Saudi Arabia. It was a difficult parting when he had to return. We don't know when he will come again…my father has been like this since.'

From Herod's Gate to the Zion Gate of the Old City can be a long walk, across the entire city, across the Islamic, the Christian, the Armenian worlds that live within its walls and, depending on how one goes, one may either just skirt or go right through the Jewish quarter too.

That day I dawdle for a long while in the Muslim quarter, eating an early dinner at the famous Abu Shukri restaurant. A vegetarian meal of crisp falafel, pickled salads, fresh hummus and 'fool'…and a quick coffee that works as a digestive.

Then past the Armenian shops…the pottery, the tiles, the old photographers. Finally a staircase that suddenly weaves up takes me right out of the crowd. I know by instinct that I am still moving in the right direction and that the narrow lane will open up somewhere. A couple of youth hostels are the only sign of life and occasional tourists step out of them—a British boy with a backpack, a young earnest-looking girl in a long skirt, hair braided atop her head and a serious, purposeful expression as she walks past without a look. Water channels run across the narrow lane as it curves.

Suddenly there is an open door on the right and I peep in. A tailor with an inch tape around his neck stands behind a counter. I pass the shop and then something in the genial face I glimpsed holds me. I retrace a few steps and peeping into the shop I ask:

'Is this the way to Zion Gate?'

'Yes,' he says, with a smile. 'To the right, always to the right.' He waves cheerily in the air to point out the direction as he speaks. I thank him but am scarcely past the door when he is out of his shop.

'You are from India?'

'Yes.'

'You are welcome. I have been to India.'

'Yes? And you are a tailor. Tailors I like. They show me that people are still getting things stitched.'

'Sixty-two years a tailor,' he says proudly, lifting his inch tape from his shoulders with both hands and bowing slightly. 'I am an antique. But I do not make suits any longer.'

'I love antiques,' I tell him. 'And if you were to make a suit, what would you charge?'

'That is a high-level secret,' he smiles. 'But come in please and I will show you what I stitch nowadays.'

I walk in into the small shop. Behind a counter there are several photographs and he points to one of them.

'See, that was taken in India. I was there at one of our churches.'

'You are Armenian?'

'A Syrian Orthodox,' he says.

He unfolds a priest's cassock, rich with embroidery.

'These are what I stitch now. For our priests here and for some who are in other countries. And these scarves which the priests wear.' On the side of the door I can see a number of brightly coloured, tailored and embroidered silken scarves which the priests would drape over their shoulders. 'I like to make things more for people who are abroad. Here they do not want to pay.'

I see a photograph behind his shoulder. He is seen talking to Teddy Kolleck, the mayor of Jerusalem at the time when the Israelis took over the entire city in 1967.

'Yes I am the mayor of my community, the mukhtar of the Syrians and Teddy Kolleck came to meet me.'

'And this is you?' I point to another small black-and-white photograph.

'Yes that is when I opened this shop. This was in 1959 and already ten years before I had been an apprentice tailor. I was single and skinny and now, now I am a grandfather,' he finishes with a grand spreading gesture.

'Do you remember any Indians who were in Jerusalem? I have heard of an Indian tailor in the thirties who was asked to make a uniform for a king.'

'Yes there were Indians, though the tailor you mention must have been before my days. There used to be an Indian who would come around on a cycle to sharpen scissors and knives. Against a flint-stone which was made to move by pedalling the bicycle.'

I can imagine that flint-stone, whirling hard and fast and the sparks flying off as the edge of the metal would be touched to it expertly. I have seen it on Delhi streets not too long ago and its screechy, scrappy squeal can still set my teeth on edge.

By now we are friends, this gracious old-world tailor and I. And as I leave, he offers me candy from a bowl.

'Take some extra,' he says as we shake hands.

And he was right about the way to Zion Gate. A few right turns along deserted neat streets of the Armenian quarter, past an open doorway with a heavenly courtyard inside, a church not open in the afternoon, a few nuns walking singly in their black habits and I reach the large parking lot of Zion Gate where the mammoth tour buses are forever unloading pilgrims.

19

'Munir, You Are a Soldier'

David Rubinger, arguably Israel's most famous photographer, is a florid, thickset man with a French beard. I met him first in the charmingly overgrown garden of Gideon Levy, one of Israel's best-known journalists, as widely admired as he is reviled across the political spectrum.

Rubinger has many great photographs to his credit, published in *Time* magazine for decades, of Israeli leaders and politicians on candid camera. But his signature black-and-white photograph is unmistakable and intensely evocative. It shows the awestruck faces of three young Israeli paratroopers staring at the Western Wall after they had taken over the Old City of Jerusalem on 7 June 1967. I asked Rubinger how he had managed that angle, low from under the faces of the young soldiers. His response was modest: 'I was holding the camera low and I clicked and I got this picture…' or some such words.

He, however, gives a more detailed explanation in his book *Israel through My Lens*:

> The area between the Western Wall and houses that were then standing near it could not have been more than ten or twelve feet across. To get the most effective shot in such a narrow place, it was necessary for me to lie down on the

> ground and shoot skywards so that I could capture in my lens both the victorious Israeli paratroopers and as much of the Wall as possible.

On developing the photograph, and being suffused with pride of victory, he generously gave the negative to the Government Press Office. The result: the picture was distributed far and wide and used by everybody without a thought to copyright, a battle which Rubinger is still fighting; on the other hand, it brought him worldwide recognition and fame as the photograph quickly became an iconic display of an Israeli victory and the Jewish return to Jerusalem.

The wall had been the lodestone to which the soldiers had rushed after they surrounded the Old City and blasted their way through Lions' Gate. They came over the Haram al-Sharif, awestruck by the quiet peace of the tranquil, tree-lined Herodian platform, posing for victorious photographs before the Dome of the Rock, oblivious in that heady moment of victory of the old Jewish belief that observant Jews should not step on the site of the Temple lest they step where they are not supposed to. More soldiers came from Zion Gate through the Jewish quarter. Yet others entered the Old City through the Dung Gate, the gate nearest to the Western Wall. At the intensely emotional moment when they found themselves face-to-face with the Wall that had been only an unattainable idea through the generations, they clung to the stones and wept, irrespective of their personal theological beliefs. At that time the houses of the maghribi quarter, homes of the Moroccans, came up nearly to the wall, leaving only a narrow passage, where the soldiers crowded and where Rubinger took his famous shot.

But all this would change soon.

On 10 June, the six hundred inhabitants of the quarter were given three hours to leave their homes. Then the bulldozers arrived to steamroll this historic district, including two twelfth-century mosques, to rubble and make place for a plaza to accommodate the Jewish pilgrims who would now gather here to rejoice and pray. The Arabs of Jerusalem naturally were not part of the rejoicing. Two hundred soldiers of the Arab legion lay dead in the narrow lanes, civilians had been killed, homes were being searched for weapons and Palestinian men were being led away for questioning. And before the month was out the Israeli Knesset would formally annex the Old City and East Jerusalem.

It is a sunny April day that will suddenly turn freezing cold as happens often in this city. But for the moment it is bright and clear and crisp. Somewhere I have read that visitors to Jerusalem often feel as if a film has been removed from their eyes, so clear and magical is the light. It is true.

The call for the Asr prayer is wafting loud and clear over the hospice. Nazeer points out the loudspeakers on a pole nearby that carry the azan from the mosque down the lane. I remember Sheikh Munir telling me that, a few months earlier, a Jewish settler in the Muslim quarter had snipped off the wires of the loudspeaker since the azan was too loud. But now the speakers are back again. And so, it seems, the battle will go on.

We meet Sheikh Munir on top of the steps as usual and pause awhile. It is Nazeer who starts the story of what happened at the hospice during the six-day war in 1967.

'You see that tower, there on the left,' he points through the mesh of leaves and branches. 'That's the tower of the Rockefeller Museum. There were Israeli soldiers there. There had been fierce hand-to-hand fighting in the suburbs outside Herod's Gate but finally the Israeli flag, the Star of David, was already flying on that tower. The Jordanian soldiers, the Arab legion, had fought hard but now there were only a few of them in these lanes and some were on the ridge of the Augusta Victoria, still sniping away at the Israeli soldiers. But they were also trying to escape. They were begging in these lanes for shelter. They dumped their arms and uniforms. They borrowed civilian clothes from the Palestinian homes in the Muslim quarter, even pyjamas, so that they could retreat into safety. The local men picked up some of the arms and tried to fight the Israeli soldiers. They even picked up a gun, an artillery piece and pulled it here into the hospice. They placed it here near the Travancore wing and fired shells at the Rockefeller Museum. The Israelis lost some men there. They also lost some men near Lions' Gate where they had entered the city. Then they radioed their air force and before we knew it the entire Muslim quarter of the Old City from Herod's Gate to Lions' Gate had been shelled from the air. That is when our hospice also got hit.'

I realize that Nazeer must have heard these descriptions many times from his father. It could not all be memory; he was barely eight years old then. But he is right about the gun. I find a snippet in *The Fall of Jerusalem* written by Abdullah Schleifer, a prominent journalist (and Sufi convert) based in the Middle East: 'Two 120-mm mortars drawn from the heavy mortar company attached to brigade HQ were also positioned within the walled city, one set up beside the Indian hospice near Bab al-Zahera (Herod's Gate) and the other near the Armenian Quarter.'

Sheikh Munir has always been reluctant to talk of that horrific day when the shells fell from the blue June sky on the hospice and took away so much. He leads us slowly across the courtyard till we are standing in the narrow corridor of shade, away from the bright sun, at the open door of the small room at one corner, the one we call the Baba Farid room.

'Actually perhaps we all had a choice of leaving before the war started. An Indian diplomat came from Amman just a few days before. He took me around the border. I could not see any preparations for war, although he was convinced that it was about to break. There had been reports about Egyptian troops gathering in the Sinai, but life was still going on normally in Jerusalem. The diplomat also came to the hospice and told all the pilgrims to leave—there were many of them here. Imagine what would have happened if they had not left.'

'But you stayed?'

'Yes, I asked him, what about us? He said, "Munir, you are a soldier. If you leave now, you will never come back here." I thought about it and agreed with him. This was where my father had stayed and this is where I would stay too, a soldier in the trenches of the Indian Hospice. I went to the bank to withdraw money. They said they could only give me 350 Jordanian dinars; all their money had already been sent to Amman. That was when I realized that some catastrophe was about to strike.

'It was after 9.45 in the morning, on the third day of the war. That would make it 7 June,' he says, each minute emblazoned in his memory despite the fact that four and a half decades had passed. 'The Israeli tanks, Sherman tanks, burst open the Lions' Gate. The original plan was to come through Herod's Gate, right here. Then the bombing started from the air and fifteen minutes later the shells were raining down on the hospice—three-inch, six-inch mortars. I remember, we later counted, twenty-seven shells hit the hospice.'

'Where were you?' I try to keep my voice quiet, unobstrusive.

'There,' he points to the room across the courtyard. 'Eighteen members of the family were all hiding in that room on the ground floor. We had padded the door with mattresses and pillows to keep out the shrapnel and the shock of the bombs. Then a bomb fell on the roof above, the roof of my father's room on the first floor. It broke that roof and the roof of the room in which we were hiding. I could only see smoke in the room. I could feel I was burnt and bleeding. Somehow I came out of the other door and came into the courtyard. My sister Amina was lying face down near this door. I bent down to touch her and I stopped. I knew she was no more.'

He is quiet, struggling with emotion. I wait, intensely guilty for reminding him of that day. Recovering, he carries on.

'I shouted, "Whoever is alive, try to come out." One by one I half carried, half dragged them from that room across this courtyard to the Baba Farid room. My wife was hit in the stomach, Najam was hit in the leg, Mariam too was hit in the stomach. My sister, Amina, was dead—she was only twenty-eight—and so was her eight-year-old son. My mother too, dead. They were the only ones left in that room. I went back and then I heard a little moan. I touched my mother, thinking she may still be alive. "Mama," I said, but she was no more. In her lap was this Nazeer, safe and sound. All those who were alive were bleeding and lying on mattresses in this room when the Israeli soldiers entered the hospice. They had been announcing over megaphones that we should all come out. We had put up a white sheet outside the hospice. When they entered, they flung aside the old board.'

I glance at the black wooden board with 'Indian Hospice' written in white paint on it. Today it sits angled on a shelf in the library.

'"Hands up," they shouted and put me against the entrance wall with several other men. Then an officer came and saw that I was bleeding badly. He separated me and took away the others. I told them that there are many wounded people here, please take a look. They looked inside and peeped into the Baba Farid room, their guns in their hands. They came out saying that it looks like a butchery inside. Someone called the hospital—the present Austrian Hospice used to be a hospital those days—and they brought one stretcher. I said what will this do, there are so many wounded here. But that was all—one by one we were taken to the hospital by some locals on that one stretcher.'

I chance across an account of the same bombing in Jeremy Bowen's *Six Days: How the 1967 War Shaped the Middle East.* Bowen was the BBC's Middle East editor, formerly a correspondent based in Jerusalem between 1995 and 2000. He recounts how, on 7 June 1967, Hamadi Dajani, a Palestinian trader, had moved his half-Indian wife Amina and three children to the Indian Hospice. They felt safe and cared for in the solid building even while the sounds of battle were all around and Israeli planes shrieked overhead, and were comfortable enough to enjoy a meal of Palestinian salads. Even as the children played in white dresses in the courtyard, the bombs began to fall.

> The Dajani family were very close to the explosion. Shrapnel and shards of Jerusalem stone torn out of the walls of the hospice blasted them. Mohammed Dajani, the four year old, was killed. His grandmother, who had been nursing another child on her lap, was decapitated. The child was unharmed… Amina Dajani saw her mother and son killed and her husband and two other children badly wounded. She rushed into the courtyard to help them. Another bomb fell, and she was killed. A Jordanian mortar position close by seemed to have been the target of the Israeli attack.

It all fits in: the gun near the compound, the bombing, the killings, though Bowen does not mention that the Dajani wife, Amina, was the sister of Sheikh Munir and the child that survived unharmed in the lap of his dead grandmother was none other than my friend Nazeer.

'We were to stay for months in that hospital, in separate rooms, some of us lying in the hallway,' Sheikh Munir continues. 'The hospital did not even have water. The local people were bringing food and water. They wanted to amputate Najam's leg and the arm of the young daughter of my dead sister. Fortunately they did not and slowly the wounds began to heal. As for me, I was so badly burnt and my face so swollen that nobody could recognize me. I even heard them talking about me, "Where is Sheikh Munir? If God loves him then he too should be dead, rather than see all this."'

'And what of the dead members of the family?' I ask.

'Well, they must have lain there for I don't know how long. I know that it was only after two days that the local people started coming out and opening shops and burying the dead. They were all unidentified and they were being put in collective tombs—my mother and sister in one, her son in another.

'Then Mahmoud came, my brother—Mariam's second son. I told him, "Go, look for my mother and my sister and her son." He looked—he had to open many tombs in the process—and finally he found them. My mother, like the ladies of that time, used to carry her gold and other valuables on her body, either near her breasts or in a bag tucked into her drawstring. When they found her, her valuables fell out and they brought those to me after so many days. Then we buried them properly. Many people came to see us, even the Israeli Mayor Teddy Kolleck came to see us. He told us to write a letter about all that we had lost. He said that they could not take responsibility for what happened because it was a state of war but they would try to help in some way. Nothing happened. We waited in the hospital, trying to recover. Najam was there the longest. For a week after that we kept hearing loud thuds as if bombs were falling in the distance. Actually, it was the bulldozers working in the Moroccan quarter. They cleared it all in days; all of it was waqf land. At one time part of the Indian Hospice was there.'

I realize then the reason why Nazeer always points out the map of the Old City that hangs in the entrance lobby of the hospice. 'It's a rare map,' he says. 'It shows the maghribi quarter as it was before it was cleared to build the Western Wall plaza in 1967.

'Well, then everything changed for us. The inner part of the hospice was badly damaged. We all moved out to the Travancore wing. There one day I heard Mariam talking to her children of leaving Jerusalem. I told them to wait, at least till the time when they could get their Israeli identity cards but they decided to leave. Ahmad came and took her and the other children away to Beirut where she stayed for about ten years. It was so ironical. She left because she wanted to escape war and the war followed her there. Later she went to Libya and stayed with her son Mahmoud who was in the service of Gaddafi. But in the end she went and stayed with my sister Hind in Karachi and not with any of her children. Hind used to work in Karachi in the embassy of Saudi Arabia. She had got married to a rich Pakistani landowner. It was there that Mariam died in 1986. There she was buried with honours; people there, too, knew that she had been helping Muslim pilgrims in Jerusalem. When I got the news, I went to get a visa from the Pakistani mission in Amman. I was asked a lot of questions but finally I got a visa. I could not reach Karachi in time for the funeral but the grave was still fresh when I reached a couple of days later.'

We have been talking a long time, slowly and with breaks. The waves of memories have tired him, depressed him and for a while we sit absorbing a sentimental dusk around a table in the courtyard. Fireworks go up periodically into a sky that is not yet dark. There is the sound of a sudden scuffle near the gate. Young Faris raises an alarm; some boys have jumped over the wall of the hospice. Najam and Nazeer step out to investigate but they return soon to say that there is nothing to worry. A fight has evidently broken out near Herod's Gate, a stones-and-knives sort of fight, and some of those involved took shelter behind the gate. Najam fills a plate of sweets and fruits and takes it over to the old man Abu Ziad who works at the hospice part-time. At other times he works on the Haram al-Sharif. He sits down contentedly on the steps of the mosque and quietly begins to eat.

'So many phases of life,' Sheikh Munir continues, in a low voice. 'The first eight years of my life here when I was happy, taken care of by my parents. Then things went wrong between my parents and I had to spend many years outside the hospice. Then followed sixteen years as the director of the hospice with the whole family till 1967. Then the last forty-three years in occupied East Jerusalem...almost as much as all that went before.' He tries to contain himself but then continues, his voice cracking. 'If you are not free, you are dead. One does not live on this food alone.' He gestures at the full table. 'And you think I talk like this to people? I do not open my heart; if some one says "Salam Aleikum" I return his greeting and that's all.'

And then he is quiet and everything, even the questions and the story, must rest.

20

A Laughing Concubine-Turned-Queen

Tareeq al-Wad is one of the most crowded and historic streets in the Muslim quarter of Old Jerusalem. It leads down from the massive Damascus Gate down towards the Dome of the Rock, running parallel to the entire Western Wall. It is used both by Muslims and Jews as they hurry to pray—the Muslims to enter one of the porticoes that lead on to the Haram al-Sharif, the Jews to the 'kotel' or exposed section of the Western Wall, their holiest site.

On the night that I write of, it is doubly crowded; it is a very special night, the twenty-sixth night of Ramadan. The Muslims are hurrying to iftar, the breaking of the fast. They will then go to the mosque to pray the prayer of 'tarawi' after the five prayers of the day.

And for the Jews it is a special Sabbath, the one just before Rosh Hashanah, the Jewish New Year. In their Sabbath best, black satin coats or striped silken gowns, with black hats or round shtreimels, they rush to gather around the wall and begin reciting the Selichot, the prayers that involve confessing sins and requesting God's forgiveness. Nazeer walks with me, as does Zaki Nusseibeh and his son Munir. Zaki, I have since found, is a historian by passion rather than profession. He was a journalist till 1997, then became a teacher of Hebrew for Arab children in an East Jerusalem secondary school. In my first queries, shot at him cold as we sat in the lobby of the American Colony, I seem to already have drawn a blank from him about information regarding Indians in the history of Jerusalem but he is a quiet, thinking man and I have hopes that he will work away in his mind and perhaps some nuggets will also fall my way.

The street is festooned with lights—red, yellow, green.

'These are not put up by the municipality,' says Zaki. 'Each neighbourhood contributes money for the lights.'

Every few yards we walk past a group of Israeli soldiers who are there to maintain peace and ensure that the festivities of the two religions proceed without untoward incidents. They stand in groups of three or four, and in a large group of twenty or so outside the Austrian Hospice. Thousands, maybe upto fifty thousand Muslims, Nazeer tells me, will pour out of the Al-Aqsa Mosque after the night prayers and the lanes will be choked as they head to their homes. Understandably, the soldiers are edgy and tense. Some show it in their sullen, hangdog looks; others desperately joke with each other to ease the hours, their guns hanging heavily in front of them.

We reach our destination—the Centre for Jerusalem Studies—in time for iftar. The centre is located in the Suq al-Qattanin, the market of cotton merchants, that leads off from Tareeq al-Wad towards the Haram. Shops line both sides of the narrow lane and Nazeer points out two hammams or public baths that were in use till about forty years ago.

I look up; the evening sky is visible in luminescent deep blue patches through the skylights in the vaulted roof of the bazaar. I have been in that suq before, relishing Arabic coffee after exploring the Haram with Çelebi's seventeeth-century descriptions in my hand, but I did not know about this centre then. I did not know of it until an email landed in my inbox, inviting me out of the blue to the iftar and a night of Sufi singing. An irresistible invitation.

We are greeted by Huda al-Imam and taken to the courtyard of the centre where a makeshift stage and a few tables have been set. She is in charge of the centre and of the evening. A smiling, welcoming, vivacious personality, she knows everybody. In fact, everybody there seems to know everybody. Even I know a few people.

'It's a small place,' Zaki says to me in his smiling ponderous manner.

A dull boom resonates in the night sky signalling the time for the iftar prayer. One of the singers begins a prayer. Another muezzin takes up from somewhere not far off in the city. The fast can be broken now. The dull boom, I learn, is from a cannon placed near the cemetery at Bab al-Zahira, where Sheikh Nazir Ansari lies in eternal rest; that is the way the ending of the fast during Ramadan has been announced ever since anybody can care to remember.

'This centre is housed in a thirteenth-century caravanserai, built by the Mamluks,' Huda tells the gathering of a hundred or so, a mixed bag of international professionals, students of the centre and Arab intellectuals.

'It was built by Emir Tenkiz,' the historian in Zaki, sitting next to me, is ever alert. 'He also built the Silsilah Manarah, the minaret just behind us on the Haram. He was the very rich governor of Damascus, famous as the man who built the water system for that city and brought water to every house there. The Mamluks were great builders; they added many of the madrasas, fountains and arcades that you see around the Dome of the Rock.'

Tenkiz's wealth and success was the object of envy of his fellow Mamluks, Zaki continues to inform me. One day they decided to resolve the issue: they invited him to Cairo and, quite simply, killed him.

Huda's tone, as she addresses the audience, has taken a darker turn by now. She is explaining how difficult it is for the centre to survive in the uneasy political climate of the Old City, where every inch of territory is a potential source of conflict. She points out the rolls of barbed wire on the balcony of the centre. 'Those are the settlers,' she says, 'and underneath, they are digging. We have settlers above and tunnels underneath.'

The Sufis begin to sing. They seem to be a family but apparently are not: six men of all ages, with the youngest being all of six or seven. The songs they sing are clearly well known. Even young Munir—Zaki's son—home on vacation from doing his PhD in International law in London, sings along as he sits on the ground near the group, photographing them. People continue to join the gathering. A young British journalist goes around from table to table, taking short interviews. A Palestinian TV crew films the entire scene. Above us the sky is still not dark, only a deep deep blue and the breeze is soothing and balmy.

The food comes: a soup, rice with chickpeas, a huge chunk of lamb. Everybody begins with the soup and immediately there is a discussion around the table about it.

'This soup is probably from the kitchen of Khaski Sultan,' Zaki seems convinced and proceeds to explain. 'That's a soup kitchen that has been running for nearly five hundred years. It was started by the wife of Sultan Suleiman. She was Russian.'

'Yes,' Nazeer joins in. 'That is where we used to get soup and bread for the Indian Hospice for many years. There was a fixed quota every day.' I want to know more but he is thin on details. 'You have to ask my father,' he gets away with a smile.

Sultan Suleiman was a great builder among the Ottoman rulers. He built the present-day walls of Jerusalem between AD 1527 and 1540. He is also credited with rebuilding the Dome itself, besides several mosques, hammams, fountains and minarets as well as the Khaski Sultan Takiya. The inspiration behind this last must have been Roxelena, the ambitious concubine who rose to be the sultan's chief wife. Known for her cheerful, storytelling ways (she was also called Khourrem, or 'the laughing one'), she seems to have been a real-life Scheherazade. Working her way into the sultan's heart, she managed to do what no other concubine had been able to do in three hundred years of Ottoman rule: she convinced the sultan to marry her in a formal ceremony. Thereafter, she removed the obstacles in her way with Machiavellian skill: the powerful grand vizier was assassinated, the heir-apparent to the throne—the sultan's son from another consort—was murdered and her own son was put on the throne. She was also known for her interest in public buildings and charities; so the story of the soup kitchen that runs to this day in Jerusalem fits in perfectly. She died eight years before the mighty sultan, who continued to write poems for her. In one of them he wrote:

> *Throne of my lonely niche, my wealth, my love, my moonlight.*
> *My most sincere friend, my confidante, my very existence, my Sultan,*
> *The most beautiful among the beautiful...*
> *My springtime, my merryface*
> *My love, my daytime, my sweetheart, laughing leaf.*
> *My plants, my sweet, my rose, the one only who does not distress me in this world..*
> *My Istanbul, my Caraman, the earth of my Anatolia,*
> *My Badakhshan, my Baghdad and Khorasan.*

We meander our way to the hospice. It is the first time I am walking the lanes of the Old City so late at night. Usually, I am told, these lanes are deserted at this hour, the shops shut early. We follow tempting detours. Twice we try to get to the Haram but are foiled by the guards both times. I am a non-Muslim and these gates are open only to those who are going in to pray. First at the Bab al-Qattanin, the Gate of the Cotton Merchants, itself. The barrier is stretched halfway down the suq. Usually, Nazeer tells me, anyone can walk up to the gate.

Even as I stand at the barrier, camera in hand, only asking to photograph the Dome from the gate, a young Jewish boy slips quickly past and has nearly reached the gate when there is a chorus of shouts from the Arab shopkeepers: 'Yehudi, yehudi.' The guards lose interest in me. They run after the Jewish boy and turn him back. With a straight face and a quick walk, he turns and disappears into the crowd.

Down another narrow lane we walk up to the Bab al-Nazir from where the gardens of the Haram are visible. Here, too, we can go no further. But there is a distraction. Beside the gate is the unexpected entrance to another hospice.

'This is for the Africans,' says Nazeer, as he leads me in. 'They used to be the guards to the mosque.'

I hesitate to enter the premises.

'Come on,' says Nazeer. 'This is Jerusalem.'

I am not sure what he means but in any case we enter and wander around the old Mamluk buildings—a large hall with a television and chairs used for cultural events, crowded apartments that have taken over what must have been an open inner courtyard. Africans came to Palestine as pilgrims to the Al-Aqsa Mosque or as defenders of the holy sites. During the Ottoman period, they worked as guards of the mosque and waqf properties, holding the keys to the holy site.

A fine-featured young man, barely distinguishable in the shadows, sits smoking with a tired gaunt woman at his side. He overhears our questions and conjectures and begins to speak. His voice is fine and cultured, his mood is eloquent.

'Yes, people from Africa came here as pilgrims, people from Sudan, Chad, Senegal, Nigeria. They came here often after doing the hajj. And yes, during the end of the Ottoman period, they guarded the holy sites. They were very tough guards and would not allow any non-Muslim to go on to the Haram. So much so that when Kaiser Wilhelm II visited Jerusalem, the Turks put all the Africans in jail for one day so that they would not stop him from visiting the Haram. These were the two ribats, or hospices, where the Africans began to stay. This was the Habs Ribat and the one opposite was the Habs Dam. That one was the Blood Prison… You will find communities from different places in the world all around the mosque. You will find Moroccans, Uzbeks, Afghans… and near Herod's Gate you will find Indians.'

His voice echoes for long in my ears—it had that quality—as we walk out of the crowded African niche in the Old City amidst the rising flavours of Sudanese roasted peanuts. I regret that I did not stop long enough to ask his name and how he happened to be here.

Sheikh Munir is waiting for us in his leafy courtyard outside the Travancore wing. It is late, past ten at night. He has not been well. A severe stomach infection saw him rushed to the emergency room a few days earlier. But he prefers this time of the day during Ramadan. The fasting is over for the day and he is at his most energetic.

It's nice to sit out in that courtyard in the balmy night. The water in the fountain gurgles in a circular flow controlled by electricity. The old olive and the Washingtonia rise above us towards the inky sky and there is the faint echo of festivities in the streets beyond.

The sheikh's wife is away to Switzerland, visiting her youngest daughter, Nimala. She has been away the entire month of Ramadan. But Najam is around soon enough, bringing tea and dry fruits and sweets of many kinds. I have had too much sweet already and too much coffee at the centre. A huge date pancake with cheese had been served for dessert and coffee had been poured into small plastic cups by the attendant in his traditional dress with a red cap. After a while he had left the coffee and served glasses of 'tamarhindi', pouring them from the long container on his back simply by bending down. It's a cooling drink made from tamarind, said to be soothing in the summer, and because of its name that links it to India, everybody had expected me to drink it. I had more than one glass. So now I decline the excellent coffee that Najam always makes and settle for a light tea.

'Takiya and zawiya,' Sheikh Munir says, 'that's what Jerusalem was made up of at one time. In common language "takiya" simply means the place of free food. The takiya used to dispense soup. It was a very tasty soup, made from coarsely ground corn. And it was not only for the poor. The rich families also used to take this soup and then they would add fine things to it—butter, almonds, walnuts and honey—and boil it over a slow fire all night. Some families took it because they thought it was a blessing, a "baraka". We used to get four buckets of soup and forty pieces of bread every day.'

'You used to get it?' I ask hopefully, imagining visions of the young Munir, Oliver Twist-like, queuing up at the soup kitchen with four buckets every day.

'No,' he laughingly dismisses the thought. 'They used to get it themselves.'

'They?'

'The dervishes.'

'The dervishes?' I can feel the excitement building up in my blood at the very word.

'Yes, in those years, there were always ten or fifteen dervishes at the hospice. Unlike the families of pilgrims that used to come, these were just single men who spent years here, sleeping, praying, going to the mosque, cleaning the place.'

'When was all this?'

'Up to 1948.'

I have long realized that many things stopped in 1948 and then many other things stopped in 1967. Cataclysmic events happened in Jerusalem in those two years; the Indian Hospice could not have remained untouched.

'Then the dervishes stopped coming. And they also changed the system of the supply of food to the zawiyat under Jordanian rule. Instead of supplying food they fixed an amount of 118 Jordanian dinars for us per year. We had to collect it from the Ministry of Awqaf in Amman and you can imagine—I would go there, stay the night there and then come back. At times I ended up spending more than I went to get.'

'And now?'

'We still get it, but we only go there once in four or five years to collect it.'

A crackle seems to come from the roof of the hospice, alarmingly similar to the crackle of electricity sparking in the rain. Sheikh Munir gets up to inspect, but it is only the faint sound of fireworks going off from Damascus Gate, which we have just come through, crowded tonight with kabab-sellers, coffee-vendors, hubble-bubbles and a man who was having himself photographed for money with three huge snakes.

'Tomorrow will be even better,' says Sheikh Munir. 'Tomorrow is "lailat ul-qadr", the twenty-seventh night of Ramadan. It is the night of power, the night of value, the night that, according to the Quran, is worth a thousand months. It is the night of the revelation of the first verses of the Quran.'

'Tomorrow,' Nazeer adds, 'people will pray all night. They say that on that night the angels are with us and all the doors of Heaven are open. God will be listening.'

The story of Khaski Sultan continues to gnaw at my mind. I trace out Yusuf Natsheh, the man who had given me a special permit to enter the Haram al-Sharif. Presently the head of the Islamic Archaeology department in the Jerusalem awqaf, he knows more about the takiya than anyone else around. He has, after all, completed a doctoral thesis on the subject. Along with Nazeer I weave through the narrow lanes on the western edge of the Haram, climb steep staircases that seem to actually go through people's homes until I come to a sunny terrace. There, in a small office, surrounded by evidence of archaeological work, sits Yusuf Natsheh. Over sweet tea, he talks easily.

'I used to gather with my friends in the early morning, soon after sunrise, to go and get free soup from the kitchen of Khaski Sultan. We would walk in the alleys of the Old City, empty except for those heading early to work, and municipal employees who, in those days, really kept the streets clean instead of just talking about it. I remember the strange shapes of the pots in which we got the soup. Some of us would take a huge pot, hoping to get more soup than usual from the ladle of the attendant. But with no luck.'

Besides the memories of his careless childhood, before Jerusalem changed drastically in the war of 1967, he also shares details of the original takiya. When it was built, the complex included an inn for travellers and merchants and a mosque with high domes and arches for praying. A ribat of fifty-five rooms accommodated Sufis and the poor. Annexed to the kitchen was a bakery, a mill, several storehouses and a fountain to provide water for the residents and for cooking. Khaski Sultan established several awqaf to guarantee the continuity of the complex and its associated charities. The income of several towns and villages used to go towards the budget of the charity. More than fifty employees supervised by a 'waqfiyya' sent from Istanbul toiled to provide the soup every day.

All in accordance with the wishes of a laughing concubine-turned-queen of the sixteenth century.

21

Forever in the Grey Zone

Just before we reached the hospice that Ramadan night, Nazeer and I crossed a tourist group inside Herod's Gate. The guide was a young observant Jew with a kippa on his head. In the charged atmosphere of the night, with thousands about to pour out of the mosque after the night prayers, it was difficult to imagine such a group checking out the sights of the Muslim quarter. They were gathered close to the green gate of the hospice and, as we passed, the young guide turned to Nazeer and spoke in fluent Arabic.

'Are you Sheikh Ansari?' he asked.

'Ibn Sheikh Ansari, his son,' responded Nazeer.

There was an awkward moment and I found myself wishing that Nazeer would hurry up and open the gate. Any second that guide was likely to ask whether the group can go in to take a look and I was not sure how Nazeer would handle it. Finally we hurried in and the group stood a long while looking over the green gate. The guide was evidently still talking to them about the place and I wondered what he was telling them, how much he knew, what impression they would go away with about the place and its history.

'There is another guide who comes this side often,' Sheikh Munir tells us when we relate the instance to him. 'A lady guide who also speaks Arabic.' One day, he tells us, he was somewhere in the city, when he got word that a Jew has entered the hospice. Instantly he feared the worst, thinking that once again some settlers had moved into the prized property. When he hurried home, he found that it was no settler who had walked past the gate but a lady tourist guide. After looking around, she asked him whether she could bring groups to visit the place. In a measured response Sheikh Munir told her that he would need permission from his superiors. He did not specify who these superiors were nor did he refuse her outright, knowing that might attract unexpected consequences. He acted smartly—that was the key to survival in this uncertain city.

Always the thin line, forever in the grey zone. The wisdom of the man is obvious in each alert tone, his eye misses nothing. His pleasure or displeasure is unambiguously conveyed, leaving no one in any doubt.

I can understand why they are so careful in exposing the hospice. It is an uncertain time in the Old City. There is the ever-present threat of Jewish settlers moving into Palestinian properties—properties where the owner can be treated as an absentee, or disputed properties. Across the hospice is a house which has just been taken over and an Israeli flag flutters from it now. The Arab family that was staying there went for a wedding one night, leaving only one sick member behind. When they returned later that night they found that settlers had moved in and now it would take protracted legal action to come to a decision about the ownership, if ever.

And its not only Jewish settlers that the sheikh needs to be careful of. Arabs too would be difficult to dislodge if they got a free run of the property. The sheikh has fought off invasions from both sides.

'In 1967 we had moved into the Travancore wing. The rest of the hospice was badly damaged by the shelling. Of course, we had written to Teddy Kolleck, the mayor of Jerusalem, for assistance in repairing the damage but he had answered, of course, expressing regret over the loss of life and so on, that the damage had happened in war and we were writing to the wrong address,' Sheikh Munir and Nazeer open this subject as we drink grapefruit juice in the small office.

'But the municipality did make approaches and we were told that repairs would be done if we allowed the Israelis to use the premises. I then went to the Indian embassy in Amman. I was told that East Jerusalem was occupied and I should not make any such arrangement. So we did not respond to these moves.

'But after five years, we were approached by the Zaka Committee of Jerusalem's Muslim community, the one that is responsible for handling the charity given by Muslims. It was headed by Sheikh Ekrimah, whom I have known for many years. I even knew his father. He wanted to house a school for Muslim children in the hospice and he offered to help with the repairs. I thought it was a good offer. I put two conditions which they accepted. One was the condition of taking over the repairs and second, that if I wanted them to vacate, they would do so within a period of two years.

'Four years they stayed and did not pay anything. Then they started paying a small amount of three hundred dinars a year. But they did not carry out any repairs at all. They let everything remain as it was, not even putting up a door or a window. They said they did not have any money. That was not true.'

'How did you manage to vacate the premises?'

'It was not easy. It was God who gave me the strength. Sheikh Ekrimah was very powerful—he was the mufti of Jerusalem—and to stand against him was unthinkable. But the time came when our government, the Government of India, started an office in Tel Aviv. We knew we could get some support. Slowly we started repairs in the hospice, pushing back the school. Each move had to be thought about carefully because this place was not just a school. It had also been made the headquarters of all the schools and the headquarters of the Zaka Committee.'

'We started with the mosque,' Nazeer recalls. 'They had turned it into two classrooms. We brought down the old door and started repairing it. Then it turned into a war. They sent a large group of people here. Thugs dressed up as journalists, members of parliament and several others. They accused my father of being a traitor, they showed him orders from Yasser Arafat that the school should not be evicted. But we persisted, slowly pushing them back. One day I got up and painted over the huge board of the school even as Sheikh Ekrimah was walking in.'

'Ultimately, the matter was resolved at the highest levels between Arafat and the Indian government and the school had to leave. The front part of the hospice was with them till 2004.'

'And the Jewish settlers?'

'Yes, that was in 1992, while the school was still here. You have seen the side entrance of the hospice. The settlers had already taken the house next to that path. One night they took over the path too. They said that they had bought the place. I asked bought it from whom? I haven't sold it. They said maybe my father sold it to them!

'I acted very quickly. Fortunately I knew someone in the mayor's office. He came immediately and turned them out, saying that the matter should be settled in court. It was fortunate it happened that way. Usually they stay and say that the original owner should go to court. Yes, it has not been easy to stay here through the decades. I have had to face many obstacles. I am regarded as a foreigner, "al-Hindi", and they all want to push us out. But I am a proud Indian and have stayed like that for eighty years.'

Nazeer sees me off at the gate of the hospice. He hesitates as we say goodbye. I can feel that there is something that is troubling him. Finally, he speaks.

'Well, this street was always knows as the street of the Indian Hospice—"tareeq zawiyat ul-hunood". An old signboard on the Herod's Gate used to say that. That is in all the maps. Then a few weeks ago, that sign was removed and a new one has been put up.'

I look up at the ceramic plate that has been freshly put on Herod's Gate. 'Herod's Ascent' is all that it says.

Another nibble at history. The name of the street is later restored with the help of some friendly and culturally sensitive Israeli officials. But not easily.

22

'Prayer Is Better than Sleep'

I surprise Munther in his shop. He meets me warmly; I haven't seen him for several months.

'Should I make you coffee from my own espresso machine?'

We sit on tables with tops of Armenian tiles. The American Colony Hotel seems deserted. But the weather is cooling down and the light is softening. It's pleasant to sit there with him at that hour.

'I don't think you could wish for a more beautiful setting for a bookshop,' I say.

'Really? I have become too cynical. I find no beauty here now. The worst place in the world would be more beautiful than this place.'

'You still have not been able to sort out the visa issue?'

'No, I am not free. I am caged,' he crosses his arms across his chest to indicate that he is in chains. 'How can I find a place beautiful if I am not free? Perhaps if I did not know what it was to be free, to travel at will to different parts of the world, it would be different. But I know and I compare.'

I watch him as he looks away pensively. He has begun to look older than before and the careless jauntiness that I always associated with him is missing.

The azan for the Dhuhr prayer, the prayer of noon, rises from the mosque behind the colony.

Munther is not in a mood to pray.

'I have a minaret near my house and the muezzin there calls for prayer at four in the morning. I don't sleep well at night and when I am about to, he begins his azan. He says: Prayer is better than sleep. At that moment I only want to sleep. But maybe I should listen to him and I should pray. Maybe that will help me.'

I buy two books as we walk back into the shop. And he hands me one as a gift. It is a collection of poems by Mahmoud Darwish. Munther had seen me look at the price tag and put it back.

So he gifts it to me.

The Ansari family is gathered under the lemon tree in the courtyard of the hospice. It provides enough shade for the entire table while the rest of the courtyard is sunny and still. Abu Ziad is walking around the courtyard, smiling genially. He has just returned from a vacation. In the rectangular garden, the pomelo tree is laden with fruit and I see the 'luqats' hanging low and ready to be plucked.

This is the first time I have seen so many members of the family together. Sheikh Munir and his wife, all his three daughters and Nazeer and several grandchildren. Only his elder son is missing, away in Saudi Arabia, where he lives and works.

Sheikh Munir looks at the pitchers of lemonade, all made from the fruit of that tree, that Najam brings forth and a full smile bunches up his face.

'O Wahiba, how many lemons did we eat, with you under the lemon tree,' he quotes from some old song.

'That's all you did with this Wahiba,' I tease him, 'just ate lemons.'

'The rest is for you to imagine, my dear,' he laughs.

But it's not just freshly squeezed lemonade and chocolate cake and gentle ribbing that sunny morning. Nazeer is finally going to take me to a corner of the hospice that he himself has never seen.

'And I haven't been there for maybe fifty years,' says Sheikh Munir.

We go past the Delhi wing where the UNRWA clinic is open and receiving patients. A small gate opens into a little crowded, overgrown garden and an old house that I had once seen from the ramparts. We are let in by a middle-aged man.

'This was a part of the hospice which was rented out by my father a long time ago,' Sheikh Munir explains as we stand in the sun-splattered garden under leafy trees. 'The man who rented it had a Spanish wife and they kept cows and sold the milk in the Old City. This gentleman is one of their children. Somehow I cannot ask him to leave.'

We peep into the house briefly. Clearly, it has not been lived in for a long time. Everything—the beds, the photographs, the fridge, the kitchen table—is covered with layers of dust and grime.

'Behind this wall,' says Sheikh Munir, pointing at the back wall of the house, 'is another small room with five or six graves. These are graves of Indian pilgrims who died here some time in the past.'

But two graves can be seen in the front garden. Large, grey stone mounds with turbans as headstones among the creepers and flowers and weeds. I have seen Ottoman graves where turbans in stone indicate that the person buried there was of some rank.

'Are these also of Indian pilgrims?'

'No, these are older. I was told by my father that in some records these are shown as graves of two soldiers of Saladin's army.'

I take him at his word. And I wonder how long these men have lain there, maybe more than eight hundred years. These graves must have been fresh when Baba Farid came here.

The small gate shuts behind us with a definitive click. I wonder when next some outsider will step into that little garden with its ancient secret.

Refilling our lemonade glasses we walk around the hospice. The back rooms have been renovated and the whole place bears a fresh, rejuvenated look. The centrepiece now is the Baba Farid room. Freshly painted, it is airy, light and welcoming. I recall the first time that I tried to go into it: my face was covered with cobwebs and there was no question of even thinking of stepping down into the dark cavernous square hole in one corner which led to the chambers below.

But now it is possible. I lower myself into the level below. There are two small chambers, one about four by six feet and the other only slightly larger. I can hardly stand up straight in those chambers. The floor shows the remains of old tiles, not old enough to be from Baba Farid's time yet old. I come out wondering how anyone could have sat in there and meditated for forty days.

A few earthen jars with spouts were found when these rooms were cleaned and these now adorn a shelf in the newly created library. The library has a new photo gallery too with black-and-white photographs from the first half of the twentieth century—of Sheikh Nazir Ansari, of the Ali brothers, of Indian soldiers during the First World War—and several shelves of books on India.

Just a few feet away, the two graves of previous sheikhs of the hospice have also been overlaid with new Jerusalem stone sheets.

And in the office at the entrance, there is a new photograph, in colour and framed in silver. It shows Sheikh Munir Ansari with the president of India in 2011, receiving the Pravasi Bharatiya Samman, the award for expatriate Indians who have done unstinting service for the country abroad.

'I did not go to a university,' he says, 'but I received this award, my real degree.'

The well outside the mosque, too, has been repaired and is receiving rainwater. A bucket made of rough rubber, as if cut from a tyre, is slung on a rope. This was the traditional receptacle, called a 'dalloo', that was used in Jerusalem. It has been brought from Hebron now to give the well an authentic feel.

Next to this well a stage is ready, a wood and iron structure covered with freshly ironed white sheets and decorated with large dark red pillows. A Sufi concert will be held that evening in the courtyard. Zila Khan, who has come all the way from India, will take the stage and sing the poetry of Baba Farid in the twilight. And when she finishes, Sheikh Munir will step up to thank her, and she will bow low and hold his hand and put it on her head and seek his blessings. There will be tears in his eyes and he will turn and say: 'Today, after more than forty years, life has come back to the Indian Hospice.'

Acknowledgements

A chance mention of a Baba Farid Hospice somewhere in the old city of Jerusalem persistently tugged at my mind when I landed in Israel in November 2008. A few months later, after I had met the remarkable Sheikh Mohammad Munir Ansari and his charming family, it became clear that the hospice was a story waiting to be written. That I gathered enough courage to make this attempt to unpeel the centuries is due to the friendship, cooperation and knowledge of many people.

My deep gratitude is due, first and foremost, to Sheikh Munir Ansari for spending countless hours recalling incidents and events from the deep recesses of memory and trusting them to my care. I am also indebted to his entire wonderful family: his son Nazeer Ansari, who became my unstinting and enthusiastic partner in this venture and helped me obtain and decipher many obscure documents; the graceful ladies, Ikram, Najam, Nourjahan and Wafa, who were always generous with their hospitality, their time and their smiles; and Nazer and Nimala, who encouraged me from far away. I would like to thank the Ansari family for access to documents, files and photographs that form the backbone of this book.

A very special word of thanks is due to Meena Alexander for gifting her exquisite poem 'Indian Hospice' from *Birthplace with Buried Stones* as the prologue.

A book that has as its backdrop the complicated political, religious and cultural landscape of Jerusalem would not have been possible without reliance on the scholarship of several outstanding intellectuals whom I had the privilege of meeting. I am grateful to Amos Oz for his friendship and his book *A Tale of Love and Darkness*; to Prof. Sari Nusseibeh for several enriching conversations and his book *Once Upon a Country*; to the historian Ilan Pappé for his books *A Modern History of Palestine* and *The Rise and Fall of a Palestinian Dynasty*; to Zaki Nusseibeh for his essay 'Sufism in Jerusalem under the Ottomans'. I thank them all for allowing me to quote from their publications, as also Prof. Yusuf Natsheh for facilitating several visits to the Haram al-Sharif and sharing his knowledge of the Khaski Sultan. I wish I could also say that I met the inimitable seventeenth-century traveller Evliya Celebi, whose *Seyahatname*, particularly its volume *Travels in Palestine*, was crucial for discovering an Indian connection to Jerusalem several centuries deep.

I owe much to many friends: Ariella and Charles Zeloof for guiding me affectionately through the nuances of Jewish history, culture and religion; Munther Fahmi for the good times over coffee at his American Colony Bookshop; Father Jayaseelan for privileged access to the church of the Holy Sepulchre; and Ravi Singh for believing in this book. I am grateful to Bena Sareen for designing the cover I was looking for and to Aishwarya Iyer and Amrita Mukerji for ironing out the creases in the manuscript.

And many thanks to my wife Avina, my companion on this journey through the narrow lanes of old Jerusalem and back and forth across the centuries, who insisted that this story be told.